C000101523

A HOME EDUCATION NOTEBOOK

Ross Mountney took her two daughters out of school when they were nine and six years old and home educated them into their late teens until they went on to college, university and the world of work.

She wrote *A Diary of a Home Educating Nobody* for the Education Otherwise newsletter and is the author of *Learning Without School: Home Education*, *A Funny Kind of Education* and *Mumhood* and the children's books *Who's Not In School?* and *The Wrong Adventure*.

She can be found on her blog www. rossmountney.wordpress.com

A Home Education Notebook

to encourage and inspire

by Ross Mountney

Bird's Nest Books

First published in Great Britain in 2016 by Bird's Nest Books
www.birdsnestbooks.co.uk

Cover photos copyright © Ross Mountney
Cover design copyright © Jenny Johnson
Illustrations copyright © Jenny Johnson

ISBN 978-0-9932614-2-8

All rights reserved. No part of this book may be reproduced,
stored in a retrieval system, or transmitted in any form, or by
any means, electronic, mechanical, photocopying, recording or
otherwise, without prior written permission from the publisher.

Edited and typeset by Jane Levicki

A catalogue record of this book is available
from the British Library.

This book is designed to provide inspiration and motivation to readers. It is sold with the
understanding that neither the publisher nor the author are engaged to render any type of legal
or professional advice. The statements and opinions contained in this book are solely those of the
author and do not necessarily reflect those of the editor or the publisher. In the case of referrals
or links to other websites or books, the author and publisher cannot be held responsible for the
accuracy of any information or advice therein and hereby disclaim any liability to any party for
any loss, damage or disruption that may be caused by acting on such information or advice.

In Grateful Thanks...

This seems like a good opportunity to say THANK YOU.

There were many home educating families who preceded me, who have inspired and paved the rocky road of early home educating, fighting for the right to do so, without whom we wouldn't have done so ourselves. And consequently without whom I wouldn't be writing about it. To them I am deeply grateful. Thank you.

Then, there have been the families with whom we home educated, and the families like you who are doing so now, from whom I continue to learn as you share your days. What a rich resource you are providing the community with your forums, groups, comments and blogs, raising awareness, increasing understanding and thus providing support. Thank you.

And to all those treasured readers who send me messages, who continue to support my work, buy my books and keep me going by letting me know how much they enjoy them; special thanks to you.

You all mean so much.

Then, there are my two special grown-up children on whom I practised and who are still speaking to me despite that! A loving thank you to them for enriching our lives.

And finally thank you to my home educating friend, editor and publisher at Bird's Nest Books who has shared this publishing journey with me making it much more fun than doing it alone.

A sense of community makes us stronger. Thanks for being mine.

Ross

CONTENTS

INTRODUCTION

LOSING THE PLOT?

There's no doubt that some days we lose the plot!

Parenting can definitely make you lose the plot regularly. When you're a home educating parent there are times you begin to wonder if you ever had a proper plot in the first place.

This book is intended for those very times.

Firstly, don't worry. We've all felt like that, even the most experienced, matured home educators whose grown up young people seem to be the epitome of success. And secondly, don't be put off by them, thinking you'll never get there—success comes in many forms and you can be successful too. Thirdly, don't feel plot-less alone; talk about it with others and you'll be able to swap stories that help you get back on track.

Meanwhile, the stories here are intended to bring comfort and support till you do and hopefully remind you what the original idea was.

When you decide to home educate you probably already had the idea that school wasn't going to be right for your family. Or you may have tried school and discovered that as a result. There are so many different reasons parents home educate; some to do with their child's well-being and happiness, others to do with approaches to learning and education in general. But although you may know what you don't want, your plan about what you're doing in place of school can wobble on occasions.

Now, this isn't a book to tell you what to do with the kids all day. The best way to find that out is to connect with all the others who are already doing it and those who have done it; research (maybe read my other books) and adopt others' ideas until you establish your own.

Instead, this book is more to help bring you back to your core intentions when you're wobbling. And give you some company and encouragement until you get there.

Your core intentions might be to have a child who is happy and to make education an enjoyable experience. They might include providing a supportive and stress-free learning environment. Or an aim to help your child achieve and focus where school failed. Or perhaps you want to facilitate a holistic education that develops the whole of a person rather than just academic skills. Maybe you want to see that your child has more choice in what happens to them in the name of education, or allow them to move away from a prescriptive curriculum and learn through their interests. Or to take a more practical, hands-on, experiential approach to learning than the academic one we're familiar with through schooling. Or to see that your child has a broad and positive social experience. Or simply to enjoy your child growing and learning and be the one who does that with them, rather than a bunch of strangers who will have less concern for your child than you do.

Perhaps you feel you want to provide the opportunity for your children to experience the joy that comes of finding out new things, finding out about themselves, the world in which they live, the people in it, how to relate to all this, what to contribute and how to build happy lives for themselves through that understanding.

Because that's the point of learning and education, isn't it? Although I think that may be a plot schools have lost.

Becoming sucked into the way schools do education is often what causes us to lose sight of our own core intentions and plot and make us forget what we want for our children within our own individual circumstances. And I guess you wanted something different from what schools provide or you wouldn't be home educating.

With so many following that mainstream path you wouldn't be human if you didn't sometimes get seduced into thinking you ought to be doing school too. You can also feel alienated from the 'real world' (a term school users will often use as an accusation—disputable which 'real world' is the most real), and wonder sometimes why on earth you've chosen to home educate.

Well, this book is to remind you that you've chosen this path because you thought that was best for your child—and you *do* know your child best.

It's also to remind you that *HOME EDUCATION WORKS*. You chose this route because you thought it would be better—and in many circumstances it is.

It's been going on long enough now for there to be home educated adults out in the 'real' world working, living productive, happy lives and contributing to society. People who have 'normal' social lives and plenty of friends. And, as someone once said to my daughter, 'you couldn't tell' they'd never been to school. We weren't sure how to take that at the time, but we had a good laugh over it.

There'll be quite a few things you need to laugh over. It's often the best response.

I've shared many of these home education moments along the way. Some appeared on my blog, some even pre-date it, before my books were published. But as it's so time consuming to trawl back through all that to find comfort and reassurance when you need it, this is a collection of my favourites, and those which have been the most popular over the years, all in one place, edited and with added material. My home educating friend and publisher told me that she had a book on her bedside table for those wobbly moments so she could dip into it and feel reassured. And that's what we wanted to produce. It's set out in fifty two stories, one to dip into each week of the year.

I know how lonely it can feel sometimes stepping away from the mainstream, even with the wonder that is social networking which wasn't around when we first started. I know personally how you can doubt, worry, wobble, cry, lose the plot and feel you're losing yourself sometimes even though you love home educating, love your kids and on the whole love what you're doing.

I've been in that situation too but there is one absolute truth I can tell you for certain; it was bloody *WORTH IT*! I have no regrets, not a single one.

It is an amazing thing you do in home educating your children. You are incredibly courageous in making the choice to step away from convention; it is truly an inspirational uplifting experience for the whole family.

When you lose touch with that, as is inevitable at times when you're tired and troubled, I hope this book will help you feel like that again.

Ross Mountney

1

Remember How You Got Here!

It's funny how things happen. I never imagined I would be a home educator. But then, I never imagined I'd have children either. How wrong can a person be?

We didn't set out to home educate. After all, I was a teacher, so supposedly pro-school. Or maybe I didn't know there was a real alternative to school —other than parents just allowing their children to run amok, as home educating appeared to be. How ignorant can a person be? I am ashamed of it now.

It was while I was teaching that I started to have suspicions about systemised education. I was aware that something wasn't right with the schooling I was involved in. And it wasn't just one thing; it was a whole lot of things really. Too many unhappy kids for one. Kids not learning because the learning wasn't suited to their needs. Disrespectful relationships. Not to mention the endless dull and dreary days that had to be faced in school.

But I thought that maybe it was just me. So I kept quiet. Behaved. And, as well as teaching, studied for a degree in education as the people who wanted me to behave advised me to do. That's when I discovered the writing of John Holt[1].

John Holt was an American teacher and writer who felt schooling did not support the education of young people in the way it should. He was one of the founders of the 'unschooling' movement to support children learning without necessarily 'schooling' and a supporter of education out of school.

His book *How Children Fail*[2] totally opened my eyes and mind. Isn't it wonderful to discover someone who thinks like you?

At last all those heretical thoughts I'd had about schooling were supported by someone else. I had an immense sense of relief to know I wasn't going insane; someone else doubted the value of schooling the way I did. So I blurted it all out in my dissertation, naive idiot that I was; how I felt schools created as many failures as they did successes and failed many children miserably by systematic and prescriptive teaching regardless of individual needs.

As you can imagine, my ideas weren't very well received by my tutors.

When the National Curriculum was implemented I felt I wanted no part of it, and I turned my back on schools and education for good. Or so I thought.

Then along came parenthood.

Becoming a parent was, and still is, an immense delight. A challenge and a delight. I don't know which is the greater sometimes, but, joking aside, what I mostly felt was the pleasure.

Those lovely soft childish arms gripping somewhere between your knee and your hip. The infectious giggling. The silky, milky smell. The adoration your children have for you. The awe and wonderment a child has at everything, even the small things we take for granted. And their insatiable desire to learn. Mine were in cupboards, pressing buttons, opening drawers, playing with tools, tasting earwigs, emptying the dustbin and trying to walk on water.

Never had I seen such a hunger for learning in anyone as I did in them. I didn't even know it existed. But then I'd only ever been in contact with children in schools, so maybe I wouldn't.

When my children started school I watched that hunger die, along with the spark in their eyes and their souls and their infectious giggling. They got infectious illnesses instead.

Cold after cold after cold. Ear infections. Throat infections. Skin infections. Nit infections. The odd thing was the infections ceased over the holidays and returned in term times. And they no longer even smiled much, not even at the weekends.

The saddest thing of all was that the children didn't want to learn any more. They weren't interested in the things we saw. They weren't curious. They weren't interested in doing things like they used to be.

What happened to that insatiable desire for learning that they had? The one that took them outside exploring in the muckiest places. The one that had them fiddling with the things in the house. And what happened to their joy and interest in life and its potential for exploration?

My husband noticed it too and it made us think. We began to think about alternatives. We began to think that not only did we want to see the

2

smile back on their faces, we wanted that hunger for learning back too. That sense of discovery and wonder at everything. Surely it didn't have to end at five years old?

We thought about square pegs and round holes and watched with dismay as our bright little pegs had their corners of individualism ground down to fit. We agonised each morning as to whether they were really too poorly to go to school or if there was really something else the matter. We watched the fire go out of their eyes and apathy take its place. We decided we couldn't continue, that there must be another way. We agonised for ages.

There were two catalysts that clinched our decision to home educate.

One was the morning I went into school without my nine year old, yet again, to tell the teacher she wouldn't be there as she had another infection. I met the classroom assistant instead who I knew was very fond of her.

I said to her, 'I don't understand these illnesses, she was never a poorly infant. Do you think it might be because she's unhappy at school?'

The teaching assistant thought a moment. 'Possibly,' she said. Then she looked wistful. 'I've noticed she doesn't seem to smile any more.'

That remark really shocked me. It was so desperately sad.

The second thing that happened was when I asked my youngest if she wanted me to arrange piano lessons for her. She had been playing the piano before she even started school and had been keen to have lessons. But her answer was an emphatic 'no'.

'Why ever not?' I asked, shocked at her response. She'd seemed so eager before.

'Because I *hate* learning,' she said, with heavy emphasis on 'hate'.

I was devastated by that answer. One year in school and she hated learning. How sad is that?

But to her, at that time, learning meant hours of boring academic things. It meant being trapped in a seat and kept in at playtimes when you didn't do what you couldn't do, even at five years old. It meant dull routines she saw no point to. And it meant an environment she hated, full of noise and crowds and hubbub, unfairness and even bullying behaviour. It had knocked the love of learning out of her and it had wiped the smile from her and her sister's faces.

I didn't believe it had to be like that. And I still don't. And home

3

educating has proved it.

Her smile came back the minute I told her. I'll never forget her reaction. My reaction was mega shaking—I think it was excitement! Hers is best described by the term spontaneous combustion.

When I told them it only took a split second for her to process my words. Then her burdened and serious face ignited, followed by the combustion of her limbs and whole body as she flung herself at me, clasped me round the middle in an embrace of desperate relief and mumbled into my clothing.

'Oh, thank you, mummy, thank you, thank you!'

For my eldest it took longer to sink in and longer for the smile to return. After all, she had been in school longer and the effects were more deeply ingrained.

First, she started to get better. She rarely had infections after that. I don't believe this had anything to do with her having less contact with the germs. I think it had everything to do with the lift in her spirits which boosted her immunity.

Second, her giggle returned. She still giggles now, even as an adult. It's part of her make-up. It wasn't only a childhood thing.

Third, she grew back into the bubbly, keen, interested and motivated child we had pre-school.

And they both got their love of learning back.

In fact, we all did and we all got our smiles back too.

We smiled at the return of their health, happiness, motivation and interest in the world. We smiled after the summer holidays when all the other children had to go back to school and ours didn't. We smiled as they grew into beautiful, educated young people who have a sense of self and who are happy. We smiled at the happy family life we had, the sense of working together, of being on the same side, and the bond of unity it brings.

In between the smiling there was sometimes worry and anxiety, discord and dilemmas. But what family doesn't ever have that? It's not because of home education. But I have a feeling the children wouldn't have smiled so much if they'd been in school and neither would we.

We think smiling is important in our family. We think that what we do needs to make us smile. If it doesn't we need to change it. We couldn't postpone our children's happiness as they went through school just for some distant objective like exam results that might not materialise anyway. Home educating seemed our only option for a happy education, as we think education should always be.

Despite the difficulties and the dilemmas we never ever regretted it. It was never meant to be for always but it just seemed to happen that way and they didn't go back to school. The children always had the option but they chose not to. As they grew into knowing themselves and their talents they decided to further their education at college to gain the qualifications they needed and from there went onto university. They made these decisions for themselves, through discussions and from knowing what they wanted, how to go for it and how the wider world works. And they are now both living working lives, building up their place in the world in the way they want.

All the people who said to us that the kids needed to go to school to be educated were wrong. All those who said that they'd never be sociable or have friends were wrong. All the ones who said they'd be weird were wrong too. And one revolting person who said they'd be uneducated, unemployable no-hopers was also wrong. But he was just a spiteful, pitiful, narrow minded bigot—you'll no doubt come across some of those.

So if people are saying things like that to you, trying to dissuade you from home educating because of their own inadequacies, ignorance, fears or hidden anxieties about their own children which they don't want to face up to, ignore them. They're wrong too.

No one makes the decision to home educate lightly. You haven't either —I would imagine you'll be thinking about your child's education far more than any parent who's delegated that responsibility to the local school.

So, *remember how you got here.* When I wobbled it really helped my confidence get back on track to remember all of this, remember *why* we did it, remember all those pasty, switched off kids I saw in class being failed by the system. And to remember that we wanted to provide something different; a happy, stimulating, inspirational, broad and practical education that suited our kids best.

No doubt you home educate for the *good of your child* just as we did. So hold your head up and stick to what you believe in and what you are capable of as parents. Believe in your child too. When you home educate, you remain on their side, a family team, as families should be. Schooling can sometimes ruin that.

5

Our family still remains a strong bonded team, as much as we ever were. Yep—as young people they are still speaking to us, even if they are geographically redistributed for work reasons!

I look back over our years of home educating and I really miss it. In place of it I have two super young people who are educating me. And if there was one word I would use to describe how I felt about it all it would still be that small simple word I used when I became a parent, that small simple thing I felt when home educating started...

...it would simply be *joy*.

References

[1] www.johnholtgws.com

[2] Holt, John Caldwell. *How Children Fail*. New York: Pitman, 1964. Print.

2

CHILDREN *REALLY WANT* TO LEARN

Many people approach the education of children from the point of view that they're not going to want to learn and we're going to have to force them. We've been conditioned to believe it happens like this because that's the attitude of conventional schooling. But home educating proved to me that it isn't like that at all.

It started with me asking my nine year old a simple question one day:

'How do you know that?'

I seemed to be asking that quite a lot at one point. I realised she was increasingly coming out with fascinating gems of information that as well as being new to me, were also facts I had no idea she knew because I hadn't taught her.

We were walking carefully through a prickly patch of thistles and weeds at the time watching the butterflies.

'Oh—it was on that programme we were watching the other day,' she answered in that really superior tone that indicated she felt master of all this information over and above me.

At other times when I asked her this question, amazed at how much she knew, she told me it was from the computer, or in her magazine, or from that book she and I were looking at, didn't I remember? Frankly I didn't. Sometimes she said, 'I dunno, I just know it that's all.'

'Well, I'm not sure, I think it's a Tortoiseshell,' I said, trying to sound knowledgeable.

'No, it's a Painted Lady,' she insisted.

'But it looks like a Tortoiseshell to me,' I said.

'It's not, its wings are different at the edges.' She was very sure of herself. I kept silent and concentrated on manoeuvring my legs through the prickly bits thinking, 'She isn't right I'm sure. I'm going to look it up when I get back.'

Okay, so maybe I was the teeniest bit disgruntled at all this stuff she knew that I hadn't taught her. In fact, nobody had taught her. How could she possibly learn all this by herself? With no one actually teaching her? With no one actually noticing she was learning? Can that happen?

I think I would be right in saying that most of us are probably under the same misconception; that children need to be taught things in order for them to know them. And that the children in schools learn because there are teachers teaching them things. And the fact that these teachers have been specially trained to do so is the reason they learn. So, in order for our home educated children to learn anything, we parents are going to have to teach them because they won't learn without it.

As I said, *these are misconceptions*, even if it's what other people keep insisting.

Let's think about children learning for a moment. But let's not look at how children learn, which is the way we tend to look at children's education. Let's look at it from the other way round—me being contrary, as you know I tend to be. Let's look at why they *don't* learn; the things that stop them learning.

The reason I suggest looking at it this way is because when I think of a baby/infant/toddler I immediately think of an inquisitive little being who will try its utmost, whatever the opposition, to explore, find out about and experiment with the surroundings which make up their little world. They feel, taste, handle, chew, sniff at, scrunch, seemingly destroy, take apart, squash and generally mess with anything they can get their hands on. And why do they do this?

No, it's not simply to annoy us, even though it feels like that at times. It's because they *want to learn*—they want to learn about their world. Learning is what they're primed to do.

Even tiny babies come into this world learning. As they grow they want to learn more. As they crawl they are off into all sorts of things we would rather keep them out of, all for the sake of exploring, which is really learning. They just can't help it.

Which brings me to the obvious conclusion: *children want to learn*. Children can't help learning, as long as things (and adults) don't get in their way. And children end up learning all sorts of things without ever being taught. Without a teacher being involved. Without even another adult involved sometimes. And without anybody ever noticing even.

Basically they learn to move, wriggle, hold things, manipulate toys, crawl, walk, play, name things, recognise things and talk without actually being taught, just with maybe a bit of encouragement. All right, bribery. We've all held that treat just out of reach! But it didn't need any key stages, or a curriculum, or standard attainment tests, or graded assignments, or rote exercises for them to achieve it. Or even a specialist teacher. Just caring parents, like your children already have. I can tell you're caring because if you weren't you wouldn't be reading this!

So why don't they continue learning? If they *want* to learn, and if they *can* learn things without actually being taught, what happens that they stop learning in that simple way as they get older?

It's ironic that a lot of teacher training involves a lot of research into child psychology. This teaches teachers that in order for children to learn anything they must be comfortable with themselves and their environment, they must feel confident and be reassured, and even basic comforts must first be met, like being warm, not hungry, not anxious or desperate for a wee. Fairly humane needs really that any caring parent would have met while their children were at home with them. And then their individual learning needs must be attended to.

Then what happens? These same teachers go into schools, which are a fairly unhappy environment for some children to be in because they are set up for crowd control and mass assessment not individual nurturing. Here they have to find ways to coerce children into learning things that are irrelevant to them because learning suddenly becomes all about objectives and not about the child. The climate in some schools is such that failure feels like a shameful crime instead of a valuable asset to learning, a child's own interest or prior knowledge is irrelevant unless curriculum targets can be met, and sometimes even basic human needs like going to the toilet are not met because children are too nervous to ask and teachers too overloaded to notice.

This can affect some kids so much it can inhibit their learning and their potential. (It's not great for the teachers either).

We are so lucky in our home educating community. Our children are lucky to have caring parents who give value to our children's basic need (and right) to feel comfortable and confident and good within themselves. For this is what enables them to continue learning as they can and want to do, within a safe, respectful and comfortable environment, as is natural to them.

From home educating our own, I realise now that children can learn without being taught. I recognise that most children want to learn and want to please and I believe the most basic thing a child needs in order to continue to learn is confidence.

With confidence they can achieve anything in life.

Sadly I see too much about our educational system which diminishes a child's confidence by failing to meet basic needs. Humane needs sometimes.

Respect, security, personal safety, love and encouragement are what give children confidence. With that confidence they will be able to tackle the less appealing repetitive skills they may need to practice to gain the levels they want. To tackle the exams they might want to sit. Even when they come up against a more competitive situation. They don't need to be continually subjected to the more damaging competition that comes from a sometimes threatening school environment and from some peers and some teachers.

Children *want* to learn. But they need to have their confidence nurtured and needs met in order to continue to do so.

So, I had to be very careful not to undermine my daughter's confidence in her own knowledge. Because she already knew how to learn despite the fact that I didn't teach her.

And if I was honest, my question 'How do you know that?' was perhaps not about me wanting to know how—I suppose I already did. It was more an expression of surprise and wonderment as to how incredible children are in the way that they learn things. Even without us.

Children already know how to learn. And they can learn all by themselves too, if we just trust and keep out of the way sometimes.

All we need to do as parents is keep nurturing that skill and adding to it. Give a bit of direction sometimes. Keep providing stimulating experiences and activities. Keep trusting. And always take care of their confidence.

And yes, peevish little wretch that I was, I did look it up when I got back. And do you know what? She was right. It was a Painted Lady.

3

DOES IT MATTER IF YOU'RE NOT
A QUALIFIED TEACHER?

Are you a teacher?

This is what everyone always asks when you home educate, isn't it? As if teaching were the only way we learn. And I found it quite a difficult question to deal with because of people's automatic assumptions about learning and teaching that I mentioned in the previous chapter.

As you probably know I did start my career in education in the classroom, but the trouble with folks knowing I was once a teacher is that, firstly, it makes them inclined to think that it was easy for me because I'd know what I should be doing. Laughable! And secondly, it makes people think that teaching is required for you to home educate and that if you're not a teacher you couldn't educate anyone.

None of this is the truth.

Having been a primary teacher for ten years is something I'm now bemused about. I don't know how I even ended up doing it in the first place. I was unhappy at school, nervous and anxious all the time. And I hated the way in which some teachers sometimes wielded their power over young people without respect for them. As I got older I began to see schooling as indoctrination, and irrelevant indoctrination at that.

Makes you wonder how I ended up teaching really. Except that it was one of those convenient career options the all-powerful pushed me towards because I didn't have any ideas about anything else. Besides, they wanted to tidy up all their eighteen year olds by the end of their school year.

I had shockingly little knowledge then of my true self, or what to do, or what I was good at. I just meekly did what I was told, apart from one rebellious moment when I refused to wear uniform in the sixth form of the antiquated (think stuffy) girls' school I was at, complaining that I had the intelligence to choose for myself. After long arguments with the head teacher—they didn't know what to do with this quiet little mouse turned all insubordinate—they changed the rules for all sixth formers and that was my first taste of actually being able to tread a non-mainstream path.

Incidentally, as a home educating parent I had a strong urge to make sure our children had a much better understanding and knowledge of themselves than I did and much better criteria for choosing a career.

During my time as a teacher I learnt how to do teacherish things by copying other teachers doing teacherish things, which were not always very nurturing or inspiring, but things they had to do in order to get through what they had to teach and keep control over some children who were challenging. I'm not proud to admit that I wielded my power over the children too, pushing them towards expected outcomes en masse as I was expected to do. I had no regard for whether it was right or not, or for the individuals within that mass.

I'm ashamed of that now, but like many young green teachers I wasn't experienced enough to know how else to do it.

Gradually, as I gained in confidence as a person rather than a pawn in an institution, I began to have severe misgivings about what was done to children in schools under the guise of educating them. But, of course, I couldn't air my views; I'd probably have been burned at the Chief Education Officer's stake.

My salvation, before I went completely insane with suppressing these radical ideas, was discovering the work of John Holt (see chapter 1) and realising that I was not alone. Then finally, well before I even thought of having my own children, I had the courage to quit rather than continue to press kids into submission in the name of education, making a drastic career decision everybody advised me against.

This might be hard to believe, but having been a teacher in the system did not make it easy for me to home educate at all. Rather, it made it harder. And I am not the only home educating teacher I've come across who feels like that.

Admittedly it perhaps gave me a little more understanding about education itself, although that's arguable. It also showed me that much of what children have to do in schools is not worthwhile, not helpful, not healthy even, so it perhaps contributed to my confidence in feeling that our children were better off out of school than in it. But that's where the value of having been a teacher ended.

After that, much of what I learned when I was teaching I had to unlearn when I started to home educate.

Much of my thinking was indoctrinated by other teachers at that time. Teachers who believed that children had to be taught in order to learn anything—not true. Teachers who believed that unpleasant forms of coercion (like sarcasm for example) were acceptable ways to get children to learn—they're not. Teachers who believed that some children were 'no-hopers' and unteachable—very sad. Teachers who had been forced to believe that endless writing, testing, homework, academic exercises and exams were what constituted an education. They don't.

There were brilliant teachers too; you will have come across them. But sadly it's often the less pleasant ones that have the biggest effect.

It was that type of ingrained thinking I had to unlearn, as none of it applied to home education. It is very hard to break bad habits, but I had some serious habits to unlearn. Some nasty teacherish inflection and body language for a start. And maybe an authoritarian tone, says she shivering with shame at the thought. Both needed replacing with respect and better understanding if I was going to home educate successfully.

For to home educate successfully I did not need a 'teacherish' relationship with my children. Nothing could have been worse.

Now I'm not saying this is how all teachers are. The majority of teachers are caring, devoted, interested people who work so hard for the children in their care. I learnt from those too.

But sadly it seems that the teachers which stick in your memory are the ones who do the damage. I hear that from other home educating parents who've removed their child from school. I remember it from my own school days too.

It also happens that parents are led to believe, still, that you have to have qualified teachers in order to learn. *You don't.*

That's the short simple truth. You just don't. Keep that in mind for a moment.

The more complicated truth is that children can teach themselves and that learning is much, much easier if the learner has someone to support them. Some caring, interested, mature mentor. It helps a lot. But that person doesn't have to be a teacher.

Having been a teacher did not make it any easier for me to know what I should be doing as a *home educator*, except that perhaps I'd already started to think about education generally. But once released from systemised schooling the education you can give your children is open to an enormous range of options. And making decisions about those options is no easier for me than it is for you. Many of those decisions are as much to do with parenting as teaching and I came from the same starting point as any other parent on that one—I knew zilch!

The things I saw when I was teaching in schools made me start to question and I continued to question throughout. Should we learn this or shall we learn that? What's an interesting way to learn it? How best can my children learn? What are their needs now and what suits them best?

These are the questions all home educators need to ask whether they are teachers or not. And the answers really have no relevance to what teachers are doing in schools unless you want them to. The answers will not come any easier if you're a 'trained' teacher because all the answers are *personal to your child.* Just like education should be.

The thing that makes you well equipped to educate your children is to do with *caring* rather than teaching. It is being a parent who's prepared to learn a little too.

If we think back to when our children are small, pre-school, we managed to teach them—or rather to develop in them—an enormous number of skills. With our help they learned to walk, talk, use the loo, feed themselves, dress themselves, probably use the computer too…all manner of things. We showed them the things around them, we showed them how to do things and we showed them the wider world. We were already giving them information and showing them how to apply it.

Home educating your child is nothing more than an extension of that.

As a parent you have already started encouraging your child to develop skills and acquire knowledge. That's all education is; the continuing process of encouraging your child to learn about the world, how they fit into it and how to relate to people, as you no doubt are already doing.

There is no reason why you cannot go on doing that without any 'teaching training' at all. The skills and knowledge children need may become a little more challenging, sophisticated and complicated, but then parenting is already challenging and you've managed it so far. You can manage home educating. You can always find help with the bits you find difficult. You can learn together—it sets a great example. Nearly everything, including support, is only a bit of research or networking away.

Teachers and teaching in the way that we normally understand them are not necessary to home educate. You don't need to be a teacher and in many ways it's a hindrance, as I found.

All you need to be is what you already are or you wouldn't be bothering to read this. All you need to be is a caring, interested, questioning, engaged parent, who is also willing to learn.

And what a great example you will be setting as such.

4

LEARNING HAPPENS FROM LIVING - NOT NECESSARILY FROM SCHOOLING

Sometimes when we were home educating I got the feeling that education was taking over my life.

I remember one incident when I felt rather near the end of my tether. There was actually more than one, but this sticks in my mind because of the poo.

Not only was the meal late and everyone starved to the point of tantrums, but also I was eating it with a fork covered in wax, I'd had to drain the pasta in a sink which was purple with dye, and eat off a table with bird poo on it.

It wasn't fresh bird poo I hasten to add. Actually it wasn't poo at all, it just put me in mind of it.

It was an owl pellet lovingly carried home like treasure, to be dissected and examined and crooned over after the boring exercise of having dinner was out of the way. But, bird poo or not, it was the last straw and I wasn't enjoying looking at it while I sat chewing in moody silence, trying not to give in to the feeling of mounting irritation.

My youngest gobbled her dinner down as fast as possible so she could get her hands on it. She was just itching to take it apart. She wriggled about, shoving pasta down her throat like there was no tomorrow and throwing her water into her mouth in one gulp.

'Finished!' she exclaimed. 'Can I do it now?'

'No!' the rest of us shouted in unison with our mouths full and our plates only half empty.

'Dohhh!' She sat and sulked, her impatient eye flicking between our dwindling meal and the pellet. 'She's deliberately taking a long time,' she said of her sister. We ignored the comment and kept on eating.

The minute we'd all finished she whipped our plates away in a whirlwind of rare helpfulness and pounced on the pellet with a pair of tweezers.

We gave up. We'd gone off pudding anyway and everything seemed to taste of melted candle wax (we had been doing batik earlier). The rest of the family drifted away from what they considered to be the most disgusting member of the household and she and I started the dissecting.

The pellet was indeed a treasure. My irritation was forgotten and I became as absorbed in the examination as she was; it was fascinating.

There were stones, shells, bones, fish scales, bits of shellfish, a beetle—in pieces. Putting it together was fun, fur and hair. We were so enthusiastic that the others came back and took part and we were soon fighting over who was going to excavate the next gem. We wouldn't have missed it for the world. Who needed pudding when we'd got the excitement of learning and discovery going on?

How often did learning get this exciting in school?

The trouble with organised education, conducted by people who are bound by so many constructs, is that so many wonderful but incidental opportunities to engage and educate during every day life and interactions are completely missed.

Education and real life do not need to be separate from one another. Most learning does not come from teaching. As John Holt said in his magazine *Growing Without Schooling*, 'Learning is not the product of teaching. Learning is the product of the activity of learners'.[1]

Learning really does go on all the time. All of life is important to a child's learning and education. And much is lost when people try to compartmentalise learning into neat little outcomes, as schools have to do, and force children to be taught rather than trust that they can learn anyway.

Also, many children are put off learning completely by schools and institutions like them trying to fragment education away from real life and force it into different strait-jackets in order to teach and measure.

They fragment by subject and content, by levels and ability, by age, by standards and testing, by time and period, and by clustering people together. They segregate learning from life by the very action of removing children from real experience and experimentation and confining them in a situation that has no equivalent in the real world outside at all. And we are made to believe that learning cannot happen without teaching, which is not the case at all. Home learning can and does happen successfully without all these restrictions.

Out in that real world, learning and education takes place by the simple act of living a life and being exposed to all manner of things, bird poo and owl pellets included.

What a loss it would have been if, when we were out on our walk, we hadn't collected the owl pellet simply because it wasn't our objective; we were supposed to be having our exercise. Or if I'd said we couldn't dissect it because it wasn't on our timetable and we had to do reading right now.

All right, I admit I did want my dinner first and so did the other members of the family. There may have been a more appropriate time and place for this activity. But my point is that restricting learning to what we're 'supposed' to be doing at the time, in other words compartmentalising it with rigid rules, misses out on so much. It also devalues the learning the children are interested in and suggests that it is only planned, taught learning that is of value.

What an excellent and valuable learning opportunity would have been lost if I'd dismissed this activity just then because it wasn't what I wanted to teach them. Not only the opportunity to learn about science and the life of a species, but the opportunity to develop in the children something very special; *a love of learning* and finding out just for the *pleasure* of it.

This is what learning without teaching and schooling becomes; *learning simply for the pleasure and fascination of discovery and knowledge.*

What a loss it would have been if I didn't answer at the time those inquisitive questions that came at me constantly; in the car; in the supermarket; at bedtime; even when she was sitting on the toilet, just because that subject wasn't on our timetable just then. Or if I stopped the natural curiosity by saying the child was too young, or too old, or too slow a learner. Or, even more bizarre, wasn't wearing the right uniform, or in the right room, or sitting in the right position. Or if I withheld information because another bit hadn't been learned yet and I was in charge of the teaching schedule.

How ridiculous that all seems in comparison to just living an educational life. As all life surely is.

I am not saying there is no place for any kind of structure. Of course there is. Most people have some kind of self-imposed structure in their day, in their home education, and for successful interaction with society.

But to separate children from real life experiences and opportunities for incidental learning, and to impose so many restrictions on what they should do, and how and when they should do it, is to miss out on a wealth of opportunity and, at its worst, to kill their curiosity and enthusiasm for learning stone dead.

It's that curiosity and enthusiasm that produces educated young people, *not* teaching or schooling. So on days when you're having a wobble about not teaching them anything, or them not learning anything, it helps to keep this in mind.

By living a busy life, learning happens all the time. This is education with real meaning. For all of us, children and adults alike.

Education wasn't taking over my life—it *was* my life, still is and always will be and that's also true of my grown up young people who enjoy learning about stuff just as much as ever, even though they're both over twenty now. They're always looking up stuff on the wonder that is Google just out of curiosity and know far more than me.

Although, I do admit to feeling at the time that there may have been one rule I would have liked to apply: no bird poo or owl pellets on the table while I ate my dinner!

References
[1] *Growing Without Schooling* magazine, no. 40 (1984).
Quote taken from www.en.wikiquote.org/wiki/John_Holt. Accessed 6/4/2016.

5

NOT-AT-HOME EDUCATION

We weren't long into our home educating life when it dawned on me that *home* educated is a completely misleading name to apply to those children educated out of school.

The word 'home' tends to give folks the wrong impression. It makes it sound domestic and housebound. It makes it sound like children are forever attached to their parent's umbilical cords. Or that they're stuck indoors all day seeing no one. Or that all learning takes place in the home, which would appear to others to be incredibly dull.

Whereas for our family, and for many of the other home-educating families I met, the complete opposite was true. We were forever *out-*educating. And it actually got to the point where we had to make time to be at home just to get something more academic done.

This was because so much of the education that takes place when children are home educated does so out in the wider world, rather than just at home.

One particular day illustrates a brilliant example. We went out to meet the home educating group we belonged to where there were a variety of activities planned for the morning in the resource room the group hired for the purpose. Usually these were led by one or two parents and their children with others assisting where necessary and everyone helped all the children, whatever they were doing. Older children helped young ones too, and helped look after pre-schoolers. Everyone just mixed in and it usually created a stimulating buzz of activity and involvement in the room.

On this particular occasion a group of the older children had also organised a 'Bring and Buy' sale to raise money for an appeal. So there was even more action that usual going on that day. The children went outside talked to passers-by and invited them in to the sale, many of them looking surprised and delighted to see such a busy, polite, conversant and involved group of children—I didn't make that up; they said so. It was a very busy morning.

We were also really lucky in that the venue had ample outdoor space and playgrounds that families could take advantage of in the afternoon. As children finished the activity they could go out for some exercise and fresh air. There were enough older children and parents to see that everyone was monitored safely. We usually brought packed lunches so that families had the opportunity to socialise more informally after the planned activities were finished and tidied up, so this group interaction often went on all day.

This time though that wasn't possible because there was an outing booked for the theatre that afternoon to see a Shakespeare production especially for young people. It was brilliant. From the very youngest to the oldest, the children enjoyed it.

So that was a very full-on day. And there were activities like that every week if we wanted to take part. True education out-of-school, but not necessarily at home. Although it was not only these group activities that took us out of the home.

There were trips to the library. Visits to the swimming pool or sports hall. Visits to see other home educators and maybe a trip out with them to somewhere of interest. Visits to museums, galleries and special events. Walks in places other than around home, field trips and study out of doors. Participation in workshops and interaction with crafts people and businesses, outings to specialist venues (like recycling centres) for resources and information and materials.

There always seemed to be somewhere we were going off to. Or someone who'd organised something or invited us somewhere and not a week went past without us being out of the house. Sometimes not a day went past without us going out of the house. And you're probably wondering when we fitted in any educating.

But that's the beauty of home educating, or rather, educating out of school. And a point about education in general; *education does not only take place within four walls*, with children sitting at desks, learning from a teacher, from books or the Internet.

Education happens *everywhere*.

Everywhere you go with your children will be an educative experience for them. Perhaps sometimes just a small experience. Sometimes a big memorable experience. But *experience* is exactly how true education develops. First-hand experience being the kind of education that has the biggest impact of all upon children.

The opportunity to experience and do things first hand is what helps children learn and *retain* that learning best.

Take the day I was sitting at home telling the children about Victorian school children. I was doing it so well it made their eyes glaze over!

But sitting at old wooden desks, with marks made upon them by real Victorian children and fiddling with the old inkwells, in the Victorian classroom they simulated at the museum got their attention immediately. This experience brought home to them much more succinctly exactly what it was like. They asked questions. Felt the atmosphere. Absorbed the information. Speculated. Imagined. This was real brain food. And after the stimulation of that they were then more motivated to study further because they were fascinated, could relate it to reality. They'd experienced it, could picture it, and now that study meant something. When it means something real, it goes in.

On another occasion, sitting passively being told about gravity meant very little to the children despite them looking as if they were taking it in. But visiting the hands-on room at the Isaac Newton Museum really brought home an understanding of it and what it meant. There were all sorts of experiments the children could do themselves. They could discover. They could experiment. They came alive as the subject came alive in their hands. We chatted about it endlessly and how it applied to real life.

This is real, live education.

Looking at a picture of a sculpture in a book moved my child not one fraction. Apart from the sniggering over the private parts of course. But standing under the very same sculpture for real she found awesome. She was stunned. Eyes shining. She never forgot it. She talked about it afterwards and referred back to it in relation to other things she was doing.

Learning about plants from the science workbook we had at home bored her rigid. Going out into the garden and gathering them and actually dissecting them for herself and seeing the real pieces made all the difference. Not to mention trips to see rare, special and really awesome ones in a hothouse. But just as fascinating were the little tiny ones we saw at the garden centre, or that we discovered for ourselves right down among the grass.

So there is educational value even in what you'd think are the most insignificant outings, if you just get away from the idea that education can only ever be delivered within four walls.

When you take them out of those walls it engages all their senses, making the experience more memorable and retained. And it isn't only the 'cultural' trips that are educative. That's another misconception we sometimes have. Even the duller trips can be useful too.

For example, something as mundane as doing the weekly shop gives children not only the opportunity to expand their understanding of money and numbers, but also promotes other skills such as decision making, observation, budgeting, comparison, interaction with others and problem solving. They can practice looking at materials and their uses, understanding weights and quantities and volume, looking at food sources both nutritionally and geographically. They can examine ingredients and discuss their effects on our health, look at packaging and its design and impact on the environment. Conversation promotes language development as much as any writing or reading.

Okay, sometimes you just want to get the job done, but you see what I mean.

There's no need to worry that because this type of learning is not structured or academic it is therefore not valid or developmental. All the children I know, who learnt by this out-and-about method, went on to polish up their academic skills and gain qualifications and entrance to college, university or work later on.

All the time, all around, there are opportunities to learn. Observation, questioning, assessing and conversation are invaluable life skills. Talking about things as they are experienced is an invaluable learning opportunity—and that can take place anywhere.

Children absorb this type of learning like a sponge. Give them a workbook and many will switch off. Take them somewhere and their attention immediately perks up.

Whatever they are experiencing out of the home they'll be learning something from it, even if it isn't apparent to you. Experience promotes discussion. Discussion promotes thinking. Discussion and thinking promote essential mental development which leads to education.

I can't help thinking about all the children stuck within the four walls of a classroom for days on end, removed from the world where it's all happening, with very few first hand experiences, and even fewer opportunities for discussion and thinking. I can't help thinking about all the people who say that their real education took place after they *left* school.

No surprise there!

Going to the park, going on holiday, all forms of travelling, a simple walk, visiting relatives...these are all educative possibilities. Let the children experience them, think about them, question them, talk about them—at the time and later. It's all out-of-school learning. It all contributes to a child becoming educated.

A final example; I was sitting on the bus once with one of my daughters when she was still quite young. The traffic was at a standstill and we were looking in the lighted windows when she suddenly pointed to the toyshop and said, 'Look at that. Fifty percent off. Does that mean...'

She thought for a second. '...if the price of a toy was one pound I'd only have to spend fifty pence?'

I looked at her in amazement and thought, 'Funny, I don't ever remember sitting at home with her doing anything about percentages.'

Home was only a small part of our children's education. It is definitely the wrong phrase. I think out-and-about education is much more appropriate.

So don't be deceived by the word *home*. Deceived into perhaps thinking it is cloistered and mumsy. It's far from it.

And when you're having a bad day, just get out for a walk or whatever and chat together. Something educative is bound to transpire from it, even if it's just how to deal with a bad day!

6

SOCIALISATION, FRIENDSHIPS
AND ONE BIG PARTY

It was one of our home education group's Christmas parties that really confirmed it for me; that one of the biggest myths about home educated children was just that—a true myth.

It was the 'socialisation' myth; that children won't become socialised if they don't go to school.

For three hours I'd watched over fifty children from toddlers to teens and from all different backgrounds clustered in a room together—a not very big room at that—and get on together happily. There was no falling out. No tears. No bitching. No competitiveness, no one-up-man-ship (not even from the adults). Everyone was happy. Everyone just got on. Together. An achievement or what?

Now that's what I call socialisation.

This is something that's always at the top of the FAQs about home educating and something parents new to home education worry about; what about socialisation and friends?

This has always seemed a rather bizarre question to me because it makes several assumptions that when examined turn out to need a little rethinking.

Let's start by thinking a minute about what we mean by the word 'socialisation'. We probably are thinking about several meanings;

    a)   that children need to get used to being around a large amount of people

    b)   that they need to find and make friends

    c)   that they need to learn the skills to be social

Now, despite what many people may tell you, there are no guarantees that these are going to happen in a school setting. And, likewise, there are no guarantees that it's going to happen with home education. But I'd like to put your mind at rest right at the start by telling you there are many, many home educated children now graduated into the 'real' social world that are *proof* it certainly *can and does happen without* going to school. So it's not something to be overly concerned about. As with anything child-orientated we do need to trust. Long term home educators were always saying that to me—they were right.

However, let's look at those three things individually.

Being comfortable with larger groups of people

It is true that at some point in their lives children need to become comfortable with groups of others, but this does not have to happen when they're tiny, or at any time *they're not ready*. Children all mature at different rates and they are all individuals. Some are very gregarious from a young age. Some prefer more time on their own and take a while to build their confidence with others.

Home educating gives youngsters the perfect opportunity to grow this confidence *in their own time*. It is not true that they need to be forced to mix at 'school age' for fear they never will.

All the young people we knew during our home educating years achieved this confidence at *different* times with gentle parental support and the opportunity to mature into it at their own pace. Some felt uncomfortable being with others right until they reached their teens, but are now happily and confidently interacting at college, in work or in other situations.

So, it isn't necessary to force children into social environments before they're ready. This is more likely to impair their confidence than build it. It is important that *you* maintain your usual social activities and encourage (but not coerce) your child to join in as and when they want to and then—trust me—eventually they will.

My youngest was one of those children who hated crowds and 'joining in'. But eventually she moved on from that and became the most socially competent and comfortable one of all of us I would say, just by watching how others did it and building her own trust in people.

In a warm encouraging climate, where no one is being forced, children begin to feel the *pleasure and advantage* of engaging with others and build the skills to do it successfully by copying others. School is not essential for that to happen. Home educating groups provide a safe setting for children to engage when they're ready.

Finding and making friends

Children do, of course, make friendships in school. However, these friendships develop there not because of anything special about school, but purely because that's where the children are at the time. *Wherever* they are, home educating or not, children *will* make friends.

The drawback in schools is that they are sometimes such competitive environments, even threatening in some instances, that they hardly create a fertile place for loyal and fearless friendships that are based on mutual attraction and trust. Children and young people can be so anxious about belonging to the 'right' group, or if they are wearing the 'right gear' and being popular with the 'in' crowd, rather than being true to themselves. Sadly, some experience bullying too.

True friendships are based on mutual interests, mutual attraction and common minds. They're not based on what class you're in or labels you're wearing.

Home educated children find friends from all the other places kids are. From clubs, activities, family gatherings, the Internet, gaming, parks and the neighbourhood. From youth clubs, holidays, playgrounds and church meetings. Just like all other families anywhere. Schools don't have exclusivity on friendships.

Over the years, as we mixed with a variety of groups, we never came across one single home educated child who had no friends. There really is no foundation in the myth that kids need to be in school to find friends.

Learning social skills

If you think about it, children in school are surrounded by other children, who are themselves immature and still developing their own social skills, and therefore probably not the best people from whom to learn them. Sadly, in my experience, some of the adult examples are not the best either. Teachers have a very difficult task in managing large groups of children who are not yet socially competent and, with the increasing results driven stresses imposed upon them, lack the time they need to spend developing those social skills. Besides, school, with its age segregation and its need for structure and conformity, is not very representative of the real world, so it isn't always the best setting for learning social skills useful for *outside* school, despite what others (usually the home education sceptics) say about it.

And what are those skills anyway? Let's take a moment to think about it.

I imagine we want our children to be open and honest and able to interact comfortably and appropriately with others without discrimination whether it be by age, background, ability, interests, colour, race, which clique they belong to, trainers they have on, or other friends they have.

To be able to do that they have to be comfortable with who they are, confident, and able to trust others. They also have to have *examples of other people* behaving appropriately towards them, in a variety of social settings, so they learn to make appropriate responses in the different circumstances they are likely to find in the social world outside of school.

Children best learn these skills from *those who have them*—namely social adults in a natural social setting.

To truly learn about being sociable, children need to be exposed to as many varied social situations as they can. They need to mix freely with others. They need the opportunity to converse with a wide variety of people.

When children are home educated they tend to interact in groups or communities with a higher proportion of adults and in much more worldly-realistic social settings than are found in school. This is how they build their social skills.

Also, all family social activities like celebrations, holidays, gathering with others, are where children will learn good social skills. There's no need to worry that they have to be in school for those to happen.

Obviously they need to mix with other children. But the best type of mixing of all is where they do so in an environment where they feel no threat, with a high proportion of socially competent adults and a mix of people of all ages, characters and attitudes and from all walks of life. Where they have an opportunity to choose friends from a wide variety of people because of a genuine like and attraction, not just because they want to be seen with whoever's popular.

There are many home educating groups that provide this, as well as the wider community. And all the home educating parents I knew facilitated social opportunities for their children by finding groups of others to link up with via the Internet. As well as home educating groups, they checked out their local area for activities like sports clubs, arts classes and groups like Scouts, youth groups etc. Sometimes the kids did this for themselves.

This type of social education is very effective and it develops children who are so socially competent it is often one of the attributes that is highly praised when they graduate into higher education or work.

Finally, another assumption about socialisation is that school is necessary because it is a reflection of socialisation outside schools and the kids need to learn about that.

This is actually quite inaccurate if you think about it. It's incredibly unlikely that the children will encounter a social climate where you are stuck with people all the same age (higher education aside) and where you have little choice about those people.

We do, of course, all have to tolerate difficult relationships, and even bullying sometimes, in the work place for example. But in the end we do have choice and, if it becomes unbearable, we can move on. Children are stuck with their class group for years. And, sadly, can sometimes be victimised by staff. But they have little choice, voice, or control over that. The social world *out* of school is quite different to that, so the social world *in* school is, in fact, poor preparation.

So where does all this leave our home educated children socially?

To help our children develop socially they need to become communicative and confident. To become communicative they need trusted adults to communicate and encourage conversation with them. To develop confidence in talking to others they need to see confident adults who support and listen to them and who model these behaviours. All the home educating communities I've mixed with provide a perfect setting for that to happen.

As you take your child out and about in the real world there are always opportunities for them to practice being sociable; on the bus, in the library, at a wedding or other family get together, in a group, doing the shopping; any opportunity where they can observe, interact and learn what's appropriate; they don't necessarily need school to do that.

Parents have been conditioned to think that without school there would be no socialisation and no friends. But I've seen the most shy, withdrawn, inarticulate and socially inept children blossom within the home educating community. They all eventually find friends and become happy and popular as most children are.

Friendships are never perfect. School kids fall out with one another. Home educated kids fall out with one another. Some kids in schools have loads of friends. Some have few. Same with home educating kids. That's to do with kids, *not* to do with home educating.

I think we were exceptionally lucky in our home educating group. We all got on so well. Some groups don't manage it as easily. But that's to do with groups. *Not* to do with home educating. It happens to all groups however they come together.

No, schools certainly don't have exclusive rights to socialisation or friendships. Socialisation and friend-making happens in a social world.

I watched the children at that party. I saw them mix without age constraints or any type of enforced segregation. I saw older ones help look after younger ones. Six year olds helping two year olds. Ten year olds helping six year olds. Teenagers helping ten year olds. I saw little ones looking up to big ones as people to ask for help rather than be afraid of. I saw a two-year-old climb onto my twelve year old's lap even though she didn't know her. I saw a teenager cuddle a toddler who'd lost her toy and help her find it. I saw all the mums and dads getting on too. Anyone standing alone had someone else go up and talk to them. That's what we do.

That's what real socialisation in a real world is about.

Never worry about the myth that your child will become a loner, unsociable and friendless, which others voice as a concern to make you wobble about home educating.

For that's all it is; *a myth*. The truth is the complete opposite!

7

A Typical Day

Call me nosey if you wish, but the thing I always loved to read about when I was starting out on this educating journey was what everybody else was doing. Especially ordinary people having ordinary days. It seemed far more helpful to read about other people's real experiences than to actually have someone tell me how to do it as per a text book. Because a text book doesn't tell you what it's *really* like on a nitty-gritty basis, wobbles and all.

So, I thought I would record here some of our ordinary experiences on typical days in the hope it might offer the sort of picture that I was hungry for.

So what was a typical day in our house?

Well, I'd wake in the morning thinking about what we were going to be doing that day. Was it an indoor day or were we out somewhere? What activities were we going to be doing? I'd try to think up some exciting things to do, things to engage the children's attention so that they didn't even know they were learning. (I said try…!)

I used to get up fairly early, before the children, so I could get some jobs and my own work done while I could concentrate without interruptions. This wasn't really that noble on my part, it was just that my husband went out early and I got a cuppa from him before he went.

Then later, if it was getting quite late and the children hadn't put in an appearance, I'd go up and open curtains and do noisy jobs until they stirred. A bit mean perhaps, but I was keen to get on and I wasn't one of those parents who could home educate happily at the late end of the day. Besides, since they'd originally been to school for a bit and were in the routine of rising early, I thought I'd hang onto it as long as possible.

After breakfast I'd encourage them to get on with something they were interested in, or, if they looked to be in a receptive mood, some academic skills I noticed had been neglected. Or maybe they'd look at books, use the computer, or carry on with a project or activity they'd already started.

Over the years we tried various ways of making sure subjects we wanted to cover didn't get missed, ranging from using structured timetables, through weekly checklists, to a completely take-what-comes way of working. All these strategies worked some of the time and all failed miserably some of the time. So we'd fall back on what always worked all of the time: flexibility.

So, generally the children would settle down to do something, look at books, on the computer, playing, devising, creating and experimenting, making, reading, whatever…and we'd keep busy till lunch, having a break or going outdoors as and when we felt like it.

After lunch we tended to follow our own individual pursuits more separately from each other for an hour or so (a chance for mum to have a cuppa and a bit of time to herself) before coming back together and doing something, or going out perhaps. We'd try and get out most days; maybe swimming or a library visit, a walk or seeing friends. Sometimes the children would just play or go outside until later on in the afternoon when they'd watch some telly.

Sounds wonderful doesn't it? So easy, happy, productive, harmonious. And working like that it was.

But, before you think we were sick-makingly perfect and you're the only one having a tough time, read on…there were other typical home educating days too.

I'd wake thinking 'Oh God! What on earth are we going to do today?' I'd lie in bed stewing about it, coming up with no answers, totally bored and burnt out with trying to think up activities and ended up getting up late—sod what time it was.

The children would get up later, uninterested, and switch the telly on and I'd launch into my first battle of the day: trying to get them to switch it off and do something a bit more constructive.

The second battle came trying to get them to dress and get on with something. I can only describe this as similar to trying to walk from one end of a swimming pool to another, without swimming. Or walking in treacle better describes it because it's black. Some days were just pyjama days.

On the days that I won this battle I didn't feel triumphant, I only felt stressed. Activities were thumped reluctantly on the table, scowls all round, and although I'd battle bravely on against this attitude, nothing

32

of any value was achieved. We'd just plough through stuff resentfully and I was left thinking it definitely would have been better if we hadn't got up at all. At least I could have read a good book.

After break the third battle commenced, this time between the children themselves over who was going to be first to use the computer.

I'd keep out of it and think calming thoughts, mainly how many Aspirin I could safely take to feel better! But usually I wouldn't keep out of it and I'd end up as irritated with them as they were with each other, which isn't exactly perfect parenting is it, since I was asking them not to do something I was doing myself! This wouldn't work (obviously) so I'd ban everybody from using the computer and sulk in my bedroom for a while. This wasn't the best plan as it's the furthest point from the kettle and the Aspirin. I'd sit seething until the house went quiet, at which point I'd think I'd better go back down and see if everything was all right.

I'd find that they were both quite happily doing something as if nothing had happened (although they would look a little sheepish) so I'd head for the kettle.

The youngest might decide to risk it:

'Can I use the computer now?'

'That's not fair, it's my turn,' her sister would shriek.

Boiling point was reached—both me and the kettle. I'd head back to my bedroom, this time being wise enough to take my tea with me, not to mention the Aspirin.

It took me quite a while to realise that sometimes there are days when you just have to go with the flow. This is just as valuable; the children were far better off doing their own thing happily than if we'd all been at loggerheads and achieving nothing just because I was insisting on something that wasn't that important anyway. Children learn just as much through their own pursuits with parents keeping out of it as they do when we're involved. And it's important we remain sweet and respectful in our relationships as we've got to be together a lot and it's up to us to set an example.

It's also important to remember what I said earlier, that *flexibility* works best. These horrendous times were usually the result of me not being flexible.

Then, here's a third example of a typical home educating day.

On our group meeting days we were usually up, keen and enthusiastic because we all enjoyed it so much, the company and the activities. We'd collect together the materials we'd need and a packed lunch and off we'd go.

We'd have a fabulous morning with the activity, both children involved with it and engaging with their friends, making and doing. Sometimes it was craft, sometimes science, sometimes a visit or an exploratory walk somewhere. When they'd finished the activity we'd often go to the nearby park to play with other families and have our picnic. After that various families dispersed. Sometimes we'd stay in the playground, sometimes we'd go to each others' houses. It was a full, stimulating and busy day that we'd all get something out of.

So, as you can see, our home educating really didn't have one typical type of day. Usually it was a combination of all these days, although I'm happy to say that the second example was the rarest.

The first two examples are probably the extremes of a huge plethora of days that fell somewhere in between. And there is perhaps no truly typical home educating day because 'typical' just doesn't seem to describe it.

Home educating is diverse. It is varied. It is unpredictable. It is hardly ever dull. But then, education and learning are hardly ever dull either. They certainly don't have to be. And home education is the most un-dull and un-typical type of education there is.

That's the reason, despite the odd boiling day, it was so wonderfully enjoyable!

8

SCIENCE IN THE EVERYDAY

I thought I'd tell you a story about us trying to 'do' science—and getting it horribly wrong—then you can bypass some of my mistakes! It happened like this:

My eight year old had her hands in the pastry mix again. By this time my patience was wearing a bit thin; it had been one of those rather long days.

I did my grumpy woman impression.

'Look, will you keep your hands out of it and stir it properly with the spoon.'

She removed her hands from the mixture and wiped them down the front of her jumper.

'Not your jumper!' I said impatiently. I tossed her the cloth and she wiped her now clean hands on it.

'Right, let's add a little water.'

'Can I do it?' she asked.

I had visions of it all getting slopped in and us ending up with runny slime not pastry so I made a poor excuse, like you do when you're trying to keep control.

'No, because I know exactly how much to put in and we mustn't put too much in or we'll spoil it.' I didn't think at the time; I could have just given her the right amount of water rather than a whole jugful. As I said; control...!

I tried to make it up to her.

'Tell you what, you mix it in.'

I turned away to put the jug down on the side and by the time I turned back both hands were plunged into it right up to the wrists.

'Oh, for goodness sake, keep your hands out!' Patience was beyond thin by then, it was like membrane. It was a good job I'd made her dig the dirt out from under her fingernails before we started. She had enough under there to plant potatoes.

She clawed the chewy bits off her hands and tried to mix it with the knife. Without success, as she hadn't the skills. But, finally, we got to the rolling out stage. It stuck to the rolling pin of course and she had a heck of a job with it until I took over again. Finally, I gave her the cutter.

'Here, you cut the shapes out.'

But by then she was totally fed up with watching me doing it all and her attention had wandered. I was fed up too as it was not going according to plan, no one was enjoying it and anyway I never wanted to make damn tarts in the first place.

'Look! Do you want to make tarts or not?' I said crossly, glaring at her. The minute I said it I knew what the answer was going to be.

Of course she didn't want to make tarts. Of course she didn't want to sit there trying to do it while I kept taking over and getting crosser and crosser without her knowing why. She couldn't give a toss about the tarts.

What she really wanted, and had wanted from the outset which is why she suggested it in the first place, was just to play with pastry. It was me who turned it into tart-making trying to make it all educational and focussed instead of allowing her to have a much more meaningful time just exploring the substances for herself.

When I talked to friends I discovered it was a mistake many home educators made. Something we all did—trying to turn a very valuable experience a child could have just playing and discovering stuff for themselves into something more structured with clear processes and a nice tidy outcome. Trying to 'do education' properly.

I was trying to 'do' science at that time, following my educational agenda. Instead of allowing her to follow her agenda, which was to play with the substances and find out what they did for herself and which *is* just as educational.

If I'd let her play with the substances—and with her hands—she would have discovered how they reacted together. She would have observed dissolving and separating. She would have felt the properties of the substances. She would have been weighing and measuring, judging and assessing. Which is all very scientific. She would also have increased some of her manipulative and hand-eye skills.

36

Even more importantly, she would have probably been engaged for ages playing with it and I could have gone and put my feet up. And finally, she wouldn't have been feeling all unhappy and bad about herself because her mum got all hot and bothered and made it seem like it was her fault.

The opportunity to learn about science is all around us all of the time. And cooking is a prime example. It's all about using substances, making chemical and physical changes, mixing and separating, utilising chemical reactions, thawing and freezing, heating and cooling. In fact, many of the scientific concepts the children have to understand when they do their primary science curriculum are covered when you are cooking with them.

Unfortunately science has been compartmentalised, taken away from real life, taken away from children who have a natural tendency to question, observe and analyse—which are all scientific methods—and turned into a subject we feel that as parents we can't deal with, when it's actually *about real life* and around us all the time. It's just a question of noticing all that you do and pinpointing the concepts.

You will come up against scientific concepts with your children most days, if you notice. And if you talk about them you will increase their understanding even more. Talk about them as in informally chat, not give a lecture and make it all 'educational' and risk spoiling it like I did.

Talk about the things you see, observation being the basis of scientific study. The creepy crawlies, the birds, animals, plants, rocks, sand, sea, rivers, weather and all forms of life. Talk about groups and families, habits and habitats, classification and species. Then there are all the manmade things to talk about, the materials they're made of, where they come from, their reactions to each other, the earth that provides them, the world, the universe etc. Talk about their bodily functions, their organs and bones and blood and more interesting bits. Their diet and lifestyle, exercise and health. Then there's water and pressure and forces and energy... There's a world of basic science at your fingertips.

You don't have to be a scientist to be able to bring your child to an understanding of all the basic scientific concepts they cover at the start of the National Curriculum. Just like you don't have to be a mathematician or a writer to encourage their numeracy and literacy. More complicated concepts can be swotted up online. Also, there are some super blogs which home ed parents have kept up with experiments and activities to help you along and understand the more formal concepts.

And you really don't have to be worrying about outcomes and go and make a mess of it like I did. All you need to do is understand that children learn best through *experience*. And that experience doesn't necessarily have to be what you would call 'educational', or predicted, in order for them to learn from it. They learn anyway. They learn an enormous amount through play, investigation, exploration, conversation.

The educationalist John Holt, in his book *Learning All the Time* [1] has this to say about it; 'Children are born passionately eager to make as much sense as they can from the things around them. The process by which children turn experience into knowledge is exactly the same, point for point, as the process by which those whom we call scientists make scientific knowledge. Children observe, they wonder, they speculate, and they ask themselves questions. They think up possible answers, they make theories, they hypothesize, and then they test theories by asking questions or by further observations or experiments or reading. Then they modify the theories as needed, or reject them and the process continues. This is what in 'grown-up' life we call Scientific Method.... If we attempt to control, manipulate, or divert this process we disturb it. If we continue this long enough, the process stops. The independent scientist in the child disappears.'

Basic science—the understanding of the world around us—is something we as parents are perfectly able to help our children develop if we just give it a little thought and prep a bit first. And our children are perfectly able to come to an understanding of science through explorative play without any kind of educational agenda.

The danger is, by making activities 'educational' or 'structured' all the time we risk losing both the child's interest and good learning opportunities. This is often how children are put off in schools. Science becomes so unrelated to them and their lives, instead of them seeing it as the basis of their lives, that they switch off, as the quote explains.

And learning is unpredictable sometimes—yet equally as valuable. Science can be learnt in the most unexpected ways, through incidental observations and discussion at the time. Through those experiences comes understanding. If the children have understanding they can easily formalise that into more directed study at a later date.

I forgot that with the tart making. Next time I gave her a nice big bowl, a variety of substances, (cornflour is even better than ordinary flour for slime) and a really old jumper. And let her get on with it. We all had a much better afternoon. And the ironic thing is; I never did much like tarts!

References

[1] Holt, John Caldwell. *Learning All the Time*. Reading, MA: Addison-Wesley, 1989. Print.

9

KEEPING RECORDS – OR KEEPING ON LEARNING?

As well as tying myself in knots over the tart making, trying to 'do' education instead of allowing my child a very valuable learning experience, I also wobbled over the dilemma of recording all the learning that the children did.

At that time I was very concerned about having a nice fat bundle of proof that my kids were actually achieving as well as lounging about in their pyjamas seemingly playing quite a lot.

At first, I wasn't clear about what all this proof was about and I spoiled several learning experiences for my children until I worked it all out. Let me give you an example from an afternoon when we were having great fun in the kitchen.

That is, my youngest was. I was concentrating on the huge dollop of golden syrup on the floor and praying it wasn't going to get tramped through the whole house before I had a chance to deal with it.

Most of the runnier substances from the kitchen cupboard were getting mixed together in a fit of experimentation to see what would happen. There were lots of 'oooohs' and 'aahhhhs' and 'cool!' And lots of valuable investigation into the properties of different substances and how they reacted together. (An activity initiated from some primary science about reactions).

Not that my daughter knew she was doing 'primary science'. She didn't give a toss what it was called (like most kids in school I guess when the teachers are harping on about 'learning objectives'). She was more concerned with making the slimiest concoction ever.

It had all started with us looking for a good experiment to do. This was because she loved experiments and I got to appease my worry about me being more arts than science orientated for which I tried to compensate. Stupid really and another legacy from the idiotic schoolish compartmentalising of subjects that basically all overlap in real life, art and science included!

Anyway, we delved into our back-up book of experiments for ideas. There were quite a few websites too so we could usually find something to interest. And it was while she was mixing away that I dropped the bombshell.

I'd been smugly thinking to myself how much learning was taking place while she played. And what a shame that no one could see all the good work that was going on. 'No one', of course, being someone important who we feel obliged to prove things to, like the relatives and the LA inspector.

That's when I spoiled it. That's when I suggested that she formally record what we'd been doing on one of those flash record sheets off the computer.

Big groan ensued! The atmosphere of fun disappeared faster than freshly cooked flapjack. I ruined what was otherwise an enjoyable and valuable afternoon by trying to make it all 'proper' and educational and record it like a teacher would.

I could have kicked myself. Why did I do it?

Well—the most pressing and overwhelming reason was about making a nice educational record of it so that I had some proof my daughter was learning. Proof, especially to those people in high and intimidating positions, that education really was taking place and that we were not just enjoying ourselves. This was in the early days before I grew confident enough to realise that enjoying oneself is paramount to effective learning.

I know many parents have this same fear. Fear that one day we are all going to be answerable to 'Big Brother', i.e. the LA, and we'd got to prove that all this fun really was educating our children (because the children's wide-eyed, obvious enthusiasm for learning wasn't enough). Proof that we'd actually done something—impressive reams of paper with things recorded on them, for us to waft in front of them and doubting relatives, of course.

I soon got to be braver than that. I soon grew enough confidence to stick to my beliefs.

The deep rooted belief that having masses of stuff written down is absolutely *no guarantee* that learning has taken place; I saw proof of that fact in school. And that not having masses of stuff recorded on prim little record sheets did not mean that nothing was absorbed or learned.

And finally, just because children are having fun it doesn't mean that there's no learning going on as well.

Education does not cancel out fun. Or vice-versa

Besides, it also pays to remember that guilt or fear should play no part in education. It's counter-productive. It ruins it, just like I was with my talk of record sheets.

From my experience in schools, and from home education, I am convinced that the purpose of much of the activity of children in schools is simply to do with supplying records. There is little educational value in most of it. Certainly not in the endless testing, which of course is also about proving stuff to others.

The children are merely reproducing what they already know. Spending time recording what they've already learnt. And that's why they have reams of work and tick sheets and workbooks, proving that they've been occupied. It doesn't necessarily prove that they have learnt anything.

Learning a simple fact or concept often only takes a split second. Learning that Henry VIII was an old sod who got through six wives only takes a minute or two. Drawing a picture of him and writing down the names of all of his wives takes ages, especially if you're a slow writer, stuck in a classroom with thirty distractions, and would rather be doing something else anyway.

I saw my children learn and retain more from a half hour programme on history or from lying on the carpet reading *Horrible Histories*, than they ever did by laboriously writing it all down.

Sometimes recording stuff helps the learner, with memory and classification and skills. But much of the recording children do in schools has nothing to do with that. It is rarely to do with learning something *new*. It is more about what *has* been learnt—and proving that to someone else. It doesn't move the learner on in any way. All of this recording, copying, regurgitating information and filling in record sheets and practice sheets is not about learning or practising half of the time. It is about *producing* something, *anything*—and lots of it—so that teachers, heads, schools, LAs and parents can feel that the children have been busy. So they can justify their time. The *value* of that busyness cunningly disguised by the amount.

And schools also seem to be paying lip service to people's ingrained beliefs that education doesn't come from enjoying yourself. When actually it can. And does!

Even when you're enjoying yourself sitting comfortably in front of your

42

technology in your own living room eating a packet of crisps, there's learning going on. In fact, there's probably more learnt while you're enjoying yourself than at any other time.

I thought about that as I looked at those pretty little computer sheets with all the relevant sections to fill in. Suddenly it looked pretty worthless.

I realised it would do very little to enhance the learning that had just taken place in our kitchen through the experimentation and the endless questioning and conversation. It would certainly destroy the enjoyment of that learning.

Recording things and writing about it obviously has some value sometimes. It reinforces learning—sometimes. But is rarely essential for the *learner*.

It is much more useful to us, as parents. It helps keep tabs on all that we do with our children, but we don't have to put that burden on the children; photographs make just as good records. Or keep an open diary somewhere accessible to jot in what you do through each day, conversations included, or an online record or blog—whatever you find useful. Having those memory joggers helps you to talk confidently about all the brilliant things you do each day with your children which amounts to their education, even if it doesn't look like it to others.

But keep all this writing and recording in perspective. Look honestly at the value *to the learner* of what you ask your children to do. Others don't matter.

There was more learning going on in our kitchen by mixing and concocting and keeping the enthusiasm for finding out going than ever there was by writing it all up. If I made them do that, they would probably never want to tackle this activity again.

Children are much better off just having a good time experimenting, discovering, investigating and exploring in their own way. Most particularly, having fun. Fun keeps education alive. Fun keeps them learning.

I sorted my own records out for my own sake. I put it in educational jargon for the LA, for example we weren't 'having fun' we were 'investigating the properties of substances and chemical reactions'. Which was exactly what we were doing.

But I knew deep down inside that the fun the children were having in the kitchen was far more educational and important than providing proof of it.

10

DID WE WOBBLE?
YOU BET - BUT LOVED IT ANYWAY!

People often asked me if we had any wobbles about our home education.

Are you joking? Of course we did!

We wouldn't be human otherwise. It is human to question and wonder and review and that's all wobbling is really. Anyway, what aspect of parenting would we not wobble about? Educating our kids is to do with our parenting, whether schools are involved or not.

This is something I think many fail to understand; that the greatest impact on a child's education is from their home life and the support and encouragement they receive there and that applies whether school is in the equation or not.

But despite those wobbles we *never, ever* once regretted the decision. We saw our children grow from strength to strength and never once wished we hadn't taken them out of school just because we had a wobble from time to time.

We totally loved that they weren't in school, loved the freedoms home education gave us, to learn in ways that suited the kids, that suited us as a family.

Of course there were challenges as we grew and learnt about this home educating process, but there were so many things about it we loved they compensated for the wobbles.

I loved it when I heard them in the next room chattering away as they played. I loved the curls of laughter circling their way through the house infecting everybody. I loved the return of the children's bright eyes, their effervescence, their enthusiasm and energy, their motivation and sparkle, the ideas and innovation and ingenuity. All that died during school times.

I loved all the funny little activities they did. The building, story making, make believe, craft work, sculpting, experimenting, gardening, den-making indoors and out—and even the activities that were unidentifiable and nameless.

I loved the freedom they had to develop their own skills and talents. The flexibility their learning had, flexible time-tables and curriculum, subject matter and approach. I loved the fact we could drop everything for birthdays, for field study when the weather was good, or just to go to the beach in storms as well as sunshine, take holidays when we liked, not worry about school runs or packed lunches or homework or uniforms.

I loved it when I knew all the other children were freed from school for the summer and I ached for their shuttered little souls when they went back, doubly loved the fact that mine didn't have to go back also.

'Do you want to go to school when the others go back and see if you enjoy it now?' I'd ask them occasionally at the start of a term time.

I never had a 'yes'!

I loved the diversity; the wonderful opportunities we had to get the children out in the fresh air when it was sunny, stay indoors snugly when the weather was desperate and not worry whether they were well enough to go to school of a morning when they'd got rotten colds. I loved the opportunity we had to go and play in the snow when it fell and come in and cook hot meals together afterwards, learning about nutrition and health exactly when it was relevant, and shut ourselves by the fireside with books.

I loved home educating. I loved being a home educating parent. Took some getting used to, but I definitely preferred it to being the parent of a child in school. I loved it more than I found it problematic, for of course it is problematic. But so is everything associated with being a parent. Is there any relationship that is not problematic?

I loved it despite the problems. Just as I loved my children despite the stress they caused me! Still love them despite them being over twenty. They still cause me stress, but no doubt I cause them some too.

Home educating just seemed to work well for us. It worked well for our circumstances. It worked out right for our personalities. And I felt incredibly, incredibly lucky.

But there's an admission; as with anything, it wasn't unfaltering. There were times I doubted—usually when I got tied up with comparisons with school. There were times I wanted to do something else, but that's parenting for you—you're stuck with it.

There were times when I worried myself sick. Times I worried that the children were not achieving anything—but that turned out to be irrational thinking.

Times when we were at loggerheads—but that's family life for you.

Times when I felt depressed and desperate and at the end of my tether. Times when I felt I was in danger of becoming insane. But that's the nature of being a mum I think and more to do with me managing my personality and own time than home educating itself. I loved home educating through all that.

I would always have stopped if I got to the point where I personally couldn't have coped any longer. Or if the children seemed permanently unhappy, or they wanted to go to school. Or our personal situation had changed. I would always have stopped if the situation hadn't swung back to fairly happy again.

But the thing that helped me beyond these times, helped the pendulum swing back again just when you think you really are going to have to stop, was the fact that this really was the *same for all parents whether they were home educating or not.*

It is also the same for any job you do, whether it is in the home or in a workplace. It is the same for life and relationships in general. We all wobble about things some of the time. And just because I was having a wobbly period didn't necessarily mean it would be any different if I wasn't home educating. My friends with children in school had just as many difficult times as we did.

Sometimes the wobbles came simply because I was tired. Or because I needed a bit of time in adult company, away from the children. Or my partner and I might have needed more uninterrupted time when we could talk or relax.

It might have been that I was worrying disproportionately about something academic, and talking to other home educating parents and those friends with children in school put it back into perspective. It might have been that the children needed to do something a bit different—times change and things move on—or we might have needed to parent them differently. Or we needed to go out more or to get more space away from each other, or to talk more. Usually small adjustments made things improve.

Gradually, over our home educating time, I came to realise that nearly all the things that seemed to upset the equilibrium were simply about families, relationships and parenting.

They were not exclusively about home educating.

The wobbles we experienced happen to *all parents* at all different times from all different circumstances. They happen in *all* family households and *all* family relationships. Not just home educating families and not just home educating relationships.

Everyone has wobbles, whether you home educate or not.

Sometimes all that was needed was to *relax, review, and renew* and the wobble looked completely different.

So, wobbles and all, I loved being a home educating parent. I loved having bright, lively home educated children who were free to be themselves. I loved living a home educating life.

The wobbles were absolutely worth it because I now have two vibrant, home educated young people in my life, busy working and sadly not still at home—well, not all the time. This is something I just couldn't imagine when I was immersed in the daily life of little people wondering how it would all turn out.

And the amazing thing about it is that whatever wobbles you have with your children right now, they too will all pass and one day you'll be missing it, just like me.

11

WE ARE NOT ALONE – THE ISOLATION MYTH

There are thousands and thousands and thousands of families who now home educate, so it's a wonder that the myth of isolation still exists. But it does. People still say, 'I wouldn't want to isolate us from mainstream'.

At what cost, I wonder? What cost to a child who is unhappy in school?

Here's a thought; I felt more isolated among the group of parents at the school gate who I had nothing in common with, than I ever did stepping away from that mainstream crowd and home educating.

Admittedly, it is a scary prospect to leave behind the mainstream flow of all the other parents doing the school run and the packed lunches and the uniformity. That prospect would appear isolating to those who have no idea what a big community the home educating one is. And it's easy to worry that you might be isolating your children, especially as this is one of the common accusations the doubters throw in our direction.

But worries are *not* reality and appearances can be very deceptive. No one home educates in isolation, unless they choose to. And no child need be isolated as there are increasing numbers of other families to connect to, online and in the flesh.

Aside from that, most home educated children get involved in the usual out-of-school activities like sports, dance, drama and arts groups, Cubs and Brownies and similar organisations, football and other team sports, swimming...etc.

People love bringing team sports into an argument. They seem to think no teams (or groups) exist outside of the school gates. Yet I know a youngster so involved in team sports whilst home educating he went on to study it at college. He just got 'out there' and found his team.

What people don't seem to realise is that just because you happen to learn away from mainstream doesn't mean your *whole life* is away from mainstream. That's rubbish and another myth perpetuated by those who don't have any knowledge of home education.

Isolated? Too busy to be isolated. If you feel isolated all you have to do is get out and get involved.

It's probably the Net which has had the biggest influence on connecting people. Not only is there plenty of opportunity to find groups and activities, like those above, to do, there is now also immediate access to others who are choosing a less mainstream path. You can connect so easily to other minority groups where once they were invisible. Nowadays minority doesn't mean isolation because of online networking.

When we started home educating the only access to other families doing the same was to cold call them on the phone, having got their numbers from a list of contacts provided by membership of support organisations. I managed it a couple of times—it wasn't easy.

What a difference now! Thanks to social media and other online forums families have instant access to others, can do the icebreakers via online chat, find out where physical group meetings are and can dip into a treasure chest of instant support so isolation is simply a myth.

Geographical isolation can be more challenging and some families probably have to travel greater distances to get physical contact with other groups and there will be fewer of those the more rurally families live. But if you live rurally you're probably used to that kind of situation anyway and have ways round it, and maybe it doesn't even bother you.

For being on your own doesn't always mean feeling isolated. You can feel more isolated being in a group of people who don't support your ideas than when you're just by yourself. And many children felt more isolated in school when they were bullied than they ever did being home educated with just a chosen few to socialise with.

A mass of people who pick on you is a far worse community to have around you than one or two who are supportive. Who needs mainstream community under those conditions? So if you're concerned that your child is only seeing one or two people, remember that those few can be far more valuable to him than a whole crowd.

I walk on my own most days in fairly isolated places. But I never have that sense of isolation I experience when I'm among a group of people who are bigoted and narrow minded and who have no tolerance or compassion towards those who are different from themselves.

That's why the Net is so valuable. It can connect you to others who hold the same ideas and principles and chatting online to groups of others is less isolating than physically being with a crowd that makes you feel like an alien. This is the same for children, gaming networks are brilliant for that.

It's probably thanks to the Net and the facility for minority groups to network that there has been an increase in home education. The numbers of families now choosing to educate outside of that mainstream rush grows daily. When you make the connections to these groups you discover what seems like a whole parallel universe of people you never knew existed but who've been there all the time. It's amazing to tap into that, especially if you've been secretly harbouring ideas about schooling that were isolating in themselves and your only company was traditional school users.

The Internet also facilitates opportunities to find and share resources, create learning groups like teen groups or exam groups, find answers to common problems and challenges and to never be alone with them. There are courses, tutors, curricula, learning communities, all of which offer support—no need for isolation.

You can find families who think like you, groups who want to approach learning in the way you do, have principles like you. There are so many now that there is a wide enough range to cover the diversity of approaches, ages and experience, so if one group doesn't suit there's often a chance to switch to another which does. If you haven't found yours yet, keep looking. Keep networking.

Some networks now list children who are graduating from their education and going out into the world, either further education or work, mixing and functioning normally in the 'mainstream' world, who show *no* signs of having been isolated from reality, as some would suggest home education does.

So isolation doesn't come into home education any more than it comes into schooling. I remember my school days as being one of the most isolating times of my life, when I felt no kinship to anyone there, where I felt isolated from the real world and desperate to leave school and get out in it.

Home educating is no more isolating than *any* aspect of living. It's about the group you're with, how you engage with it, how it engages with you. It's about finding the right group, a group that is open and broad minded, non-discriminatory and welcoming, which is what I found most home educating families to be.

12

READING

Goodness - do we get hung up about our children's reading!

I used to get hung up about reading as a teacher, but that was mostly because I was told to force it on them whether they were ready or not. But the other reason I got hung up about it was because I noticed that for many of the kids the systematic strategies I was expected to adopt towards teaching them to read just didn't seem to work.

I also made another fascinating observation; some seemed to read easily without it being a result of strategies, whereas others seemed to struggle whatever approach I took, strategic or not, and despite their obvious intelligence.

That was when I decided that the development of reading was an entirely personal thing that should start from the child's needs, not from a scheme. I've met several teachers who would back up that idea.

Most home educators I knew also educated their children from that same point of view. They start from their *children's needs. Not* a strategy. And I believe that's exactly why home education is so successful and exactly why most home educated children end up being able to read.

It's also why my heart sinks whenever I hear about another government literacy strategy, because they come up with these strategies as if it's the answer everyone's been looking for. But there will *never* be *one* answer for all the diversity of children there are in the world. Most particularly if it comes from *outside* the child.

What we need to do is *start from the child*, and look for an approach that suits their particular needs. Not devise a strategy and then try and fit the children to it, which is how the government expects educational strategies to work.

Instead, look at your child. Look at what they enjoy. Provide books they enjoy. Read stories they love. And proceed from there. Try not to get too anxious.

It's natural we get anxious about our children's reading because we know it's the key to much that follows. This sometimes results in us using schemes that can be less appealing to a child than letting them choose their books, creating a false and enforced situation more inclined to put children off. Enforcement is not the ideal atmosphere in which to learn.

And most children do manage it without enforced intervention, through encouragement, example, *being read to*, and by enjoying books and stories with their parents. Usually this is all it takes, plus patience and trust on the part of the parents.

I have seen many children learning to read, both in a classroom and out of it. I have seen four year olds pick it up like they picked up learning to talk, seemingly with no effort and as a natural progression of their skills. I have seen children for whom reading was a complete mystery until it clicked magically at around seven or eight. I have seen children who struggle to see any relationship at all between the marks in the book and the interpretation of them as a spoken word, for whom reading is a long slow process that never falls into place with that satisfying click but goes on slowly, slowly improving right into their teens. I had one of those. That's just the way they are.

But for all these children no one strategy or reading scheme was the answer. It never could be. They are all different. It helps to be patient and remember this.

This is also what Alan Thomas and Harriet Pattison found whilst researching for their book *How Children Learn at Home*[1]. They did much research into the subject and suggest that, although reading is one of the most researched areas of education, there has been little agreement over the right way of teaching it. Many home educating parents they interviewed said that when they forced reading onto their children it put them off.

The authors then go on to illustrate, through various examples from home educating parents, how children instead came to reading from being in a literate environment, through their various interests and hobbies, from encouragement, from natural family activities and a culture of reading within the family and the daily tasks every family is involved in.

Like us, they found the best way forward seemed to be to provide a multitude of reading and print experiences, keeping it light and enjoyable, making sure they never get put off. And giving the children their own time in which to enjoy, develop and refine their skills.

My youngest was one who needed more time. She was not a child who enjoyed reading, or found it easy; she'd rather be doing something active anyway. My first loved reading so much I actually had to encourage her to do other things at times, but the second was the opposite and there are many like her. It's important not to judge.

Sadly, if you don't read early on people tend to judge you as ignorant even though there is now research to show that there is no correlation between intelligence and the ability to read—or not.

So, I tried not to make an issue out of it, yet I always encouraged reading. I kept it light. I kept reading to my child and we enjoyed endless books together. And I never adopted one strategy. I didn't need to. She had her own.

Children adopt all kinds of strategies in order to learn if they're keen and not made to feel uncomfortable with it. And with reading it's just the same.

My child displayed many of the traits attributed to dyslexia and it looked at one point like she would never be able to decipher print well enough to be able to get something from it. And like many other parents (and it was a great comfort to me to hear that loads of other parents were going through the same anxieties) I worried myself sick in the early days that I should be doing something about it.

To an extent, that was true. But the thing I had to do about it, and what I think had the greatest effect, was not me employing another strategy, but the opposite—backing off. Instead of trying to 'teach' her to read, which created enormous tension, I just encouraged the unstructured enjoyment of stories, books, magazines and simple computer games involving words and allowed her to adopt her own strategies.

Forcing reading on children in dull schematic ways might work for a few. But in no way does it work for all and it has the danger of putting them off for ever.

Like some of the parents say in Thomas and Pattison's book, I don't think I actually *taught* my child to read at all. And what's more important for you to know is that I very nearly put her off for life by my interference. You might want to try and learn from my mistake.

Something we tend to overlook as adults, with regard to children reading, is that most children will *want* to read, just like they want to use mobile phones, social media and so on. Reading (like texting) is part of a culture they want involvement in.

Most of them don't need to be taught and this is what Thomas and

Pattison illustrated. Very few of the sample parents attributed their child's ability to read with them actually being taught. Instead they provided encouragement, observation and exposure to words, books, stories and the literature that's all around us all the time and the children developed into independent readers because they were interested to do so and were left to come to it in their own time.

I believe this happens because like other skills—using the computer, using mobiles, cooking, driving—they see it as part of the adult culture. And they want some of it. As long as we don't create tension, conflict and unhappiness they will eventually read. At different times perhaps, and in different ways. But the time it takes to do so can be left up to them.

That is the important part. The time it takes for our kids to come to reading doesn't matter. They will come to it eventually, if they're not made to feel bad about it because they are not doing it in a required time scale. What does matter is that reading is always a pleasure.

I was amazed at my child's original strategies. I was amazed how she interpreted the code of print as we looked at it together. I'd see her mind ticking over when a word threw her. I'd see her mentally trying all sorts of deciphering tactics. And the minute I interfered she shut me up— quite rightly. She stopped me interrupting her process of trying different methods to work it out. And what strategies could work better than those she devised herself?

If we want to usefully help our children to read it's best to think beyond the school confines of age, schemes and time limits, which make us feel anxious. It's best to limit our interference, be encouraging and carry on reading *to* them. It's now understood that reading to a child is what has the most profound effect on their ability to read and that we should go on reading to them as long as they want it. I remember reading Harry Potter to mine right into her teens, when she still wasn't up to reading a book of that length herself.

This didn't matter to us because we could approach her learning from so many other practical, experiential, non print-based ways—YouTube is a great example. You can learn almost anything now without having to go via print. So not reading fluently until later needn't hold up a home educated child's educational and intellectual development like it would in a school.

Our youngest didn't read a whole book until she was into teenhood. But she still went onto college and uni and had no trouble adapting her reading strategies to cope with study and essay writing (writing being something else she didn't enjoy). But she was never made to feel awkward or ashamed by us just because she came to reading later than many. At uni she decided to go for a dyslexia assessment and had it confirmed, not because she particularly needed to, but because it allowed her to understand herself better.

Children do not really need some strategy for reading, designed by someone who has governmental targets to meet without consideration for the diversity of the individual, in order to learn to read. They need *understanding and patience*, our trust in them, plenty of time for enjoying books together, a climate of appreciation of words and stories, and they will happily develop the skill of reading in time.

References
[1] Thomas, Alan, and Harriet Pattison. *How Children Learn at Home*. London: Continuum, 2007. Print.

13

HELP! THEY'RE IN FRONT OF A SCREEN TOO MUCH

'Oh my goodness, they seem to be gaming an awful lot!', I've heard many a parent say over the years.

I remember one of my contemporaries saying it was all her youngest seemed to want to do. However, he's passing his GCSEs with A stars at the moment and looking at going onto college and uni, so he was learning other things and it doesn't seem to have done any harm.

It's a concern which often comes up on the home education forums. The one about how much gaming/telly/screen time is acceptable.

Luckily for me, when ours were at home full time, gaming wasn't as big as it is now, but watching the telly too much was certainly an issue. There's a funny episode about it in my book *A Funny Kind of Education*[1] as I tried to ration their telly time. It was an exercise in patience and consistency, but was it worth it?

Well, even if I didn't manage to maintain my rule about keeping the telly off sometimes, it did at least raise discussions about why it wasn't desirable to be watching it all the time, what it did to our minds and bodies, and how we needed contrast and variety in what we did.

Basically, though, I always took the approach that too much of any one activity was generally not healthy. And, as with many aspects of parenting, we sometimes have a battle on our hands as to what is best for our kids.

Can you believe that my eldest read so much I often had to encourage her away from reading so that she experienced other things? The youngest was the opposite, I was forever encouraging her to read.

The point I made to them, though, in support of what I asked of them, was that it was important to have a balance between all kinds of activities; sedentary and active, studious and practical, intense or relaxed, indoors or out, alone or with others, and between all subjects. And screen time was included.

We spent much time talking about this and I encouraged them as they grew older to organise themselves accordingly. We weren't really a dictatorial type of family, we discussed everything and I think the children generally trusted that whatever I requested was founded in wanting what was good for them and they were happy to comply. Mostly. It didn't always happen, but you win some, you lose some. And that's what parenting's about; give and take and compromise.

However, I know many parents find that the lure of gaming is so powerful they are concerned about how much time the children spend in front of a screen and whether this should be regulated.

As with many of the approaches to home education, and to parenting really, this is very much a personal decision, dependent on your own family and individual circumstances.

We all have to make judgements all the time about what we think is best for our children. We also have to balance what we think is best with keeping our relationships communicative and workable, as they need to be to home educate happily.

And we definitely need to question ourselves as to whether what we ask of our children is more for our own adult comfort than really of benefit to them. And these all apply to the issue of gaming or computer time.

If you have a fairly structured type of approach then regulation of their game time is probably part of that structure. For those who home educate more autonomously the danger of too much time gaming or at the computer can become a real issue.

This is what one parent had to say about it on her blog at the time and what resulted two years later:

I had been imposing screen limits with the view that it would encourage other interests, necessity being the mother of invention and all that. I was wrong, particularly where my son was concerned. Instead of finding other ways to fill his time, he became obsessed with that part of the day when he could fire up the Xbox. If I'd said 4pm, then he would clock watch all day. If I said weekends only, he would calendar watch. For the rest of the time he developed an uncanny ability to wander from room to room for hours! Stopping him doing the one thing he wanted most did not enable him to come up with other constructive ways to fill his time at all, it actively prevented it.

And when he was in 'screens permitted time', that's all he would do, not wanting to waste a moment of it.

Also, I found myself faced with an increasing number of occasions when I would relax the rules 'just this once':

'Mum, my friend has texted me to ask me to play online with him now. He has to go out with his family in an hour. Can I start my screentime early?'

'Mum, I just need to go on Facebook to find out what time drama is starting this week.'

Or times when I realised that my screen rules were subscribing to a specific set of values about what is and is not 'educational' and that this made no sense:

'So, I'm allowed to check YouTube for a science clip?'

I began to see that my controlling of 'screen time' was false and was cutting them off from the ways they access the world. It was also preventing those myriad connections that make self directed learning so effective. With the high tech lives we lead, the lines between 'constructive' and 'non-constructive' screen based activities are so blurred as to be unrecognisable.

And by even thinking about it in those terms, I realised, I was judging their activities based on my own personal view of what is and is not 'constructive'. I remembered Matt Groening, creator of The Simpsons, saying how his mother had despaired at the amount of time he spent watching cartoons.

So, we now have no limits to screens at all...

I needn't have worried....two years later I haven't regretted my decision. My eldest daughter is now 19 and at college studying A Levels, one of which is Media Studies. Her passion for gaming proved to be a real asset. It's given her a focus for the website she is creating and is providing some interesting topics for her coursework, in which she is looking at the representation of women in gaming and the use of violence.

My son and younger daughter are studying for some GCSEs which involve web research and my son has found that his gaming really does help his concentration and hand-eye coordination.

There are a lot of spin off learning opportunities too. For example, one particular game (Bioshock, if you're interested!) has introduced the girls to 'vintage' music and inspired a love of artists such as

Bobby Darin and Tony Bennett. I've recently followed this up by purchasing the film 'Under The Sea', about Bobby Darin's life, which I know will lead to further discussions.

Social media sites such as Facebook are, as you can imagine, a pretty much permanent feature. Yet I don't see this as a negative at all. I'm on them too and we all have regular spur of the moment discussions about the best way to use them and share examples of times when we've seen others use them in ways that we're not sure is particularly wise. Internet safety is another topic and they're all becoming very savvy.

The key to it all has been for me to stay involved, interested and non-judgemental and keep the conversation flowing.

I think however you decide to deal with the gaming and 'screen time' issue for yourself, and it will be a personal decision that suits you and your family, this last sentence probably is the best guidance!

References

[1] Mountney, Ross. *A Funny Kind of Education*. North Charleston, SC: CreateSpace, 2012. Print.

14

CURRICULUM: NATIONAL; NATURAL; PERSONAL; OPTIONAL?

Curriculum is something I get asked about a lot. Curriculum is something home educators can worry about a lot. But I'll let you into a little secret; a curriculum is no big deal.

I found this out quite early in my home educating life. I came upon it quite by accident when I was having a tantrum about punctuation.

It could easily have been a tantrum about decimals or a tantrum about Queen Victoria. It's just that punctuation happened to be the focus at the time.

We were wrestling away with an exercise in an English workbook that supposedly followed the National Curriculum. My child at that time had asked for this workbook because she wanted to be able to do the same sort of exercises that her contemporaries in school were doing. In it she was asked to punctuate a paragraph.

She'd had a go at it. Got it wrong. Couldn't see why after checking it. I'd had a go. Got it wrong. Several times.

Now you may be able to judge better than me here but I don't reckon that my use of punctuation is too bad. But after the pair of us had wrestled with it, discussed it, become more heated about it and still got it wrong, we were both left feeling totally useless, totally inadequate, enormously frustrated and thereafter lacking in any confidence we ever had in being able to punctuate anything.

And that raises an important point the English curriculum overlooks; punctuation is a very personal thing.

A question demands a question mark. A speech demands speech marks. A full stop ends a sentence. But how anyone can govern someone else's use of commas is beyond me. I'm not psychic after all, as much as I try and lead the children to believe it about the contents of the biscuit tin.

Who knows how a person wants their bit of writing punctuated! Or should that be ?

That's when I had the tantrum. The National Curriculum does it to me every time.

I remember having a major one over trying to change nineteen twentieths into a decimal. This was another exercise we came across from a National Curriculum workbook. It had my daughter really doubting her ability in maths. Yet will it impair her life not knowing how to change nineteen twentieths into a decimal, I ask? She's brilliant at budgeting.

On another occasion she was feeling inadequate about some topic in history because she realised she hadn't covered it. Yet, this was a fourteen year old who presented a talk on the history of fashion so well that someone in the business commented that she knew more about it than her degree students.

This is what makes me throw tantrums about having a curriculum. Because it compartmentalises knowledge into a hierarchy that rates some facts as more important to know than others, which is ridiculous yet can make someone who is perfectly intelligent feel really bad.

What's a curriculum for, anyway? What's in it, or should be in it? And what's in it for us, most particularly if its content seems absolutely irrelevant to a particular individual?

Curriculum is just about content and measurable standardisation. It is basically nothing more than a list that someone (who doesn't know your child) is dictating your child should learn. It became National in order to standardise that learning across the country so it could be tested and everyone compared.

It is exactly because it is standardised and national that it's a bad idea. For it pays no attention to the *individual.* It pays no attention to its *relevance* to the individual, or their needs. And even worse, it has set up content that is so inappropriate to so many of our children that it is leading perfectly intelligent children to feel stupid.

As I said earlier, my child knows a lot about the history of fashion. She's read a lot about it. She understands a lot about political and social history because it influenced the fashion of the time. She is an intelligent child who has shown an aptitude for research and study.

But she hasn't studied the Anglo Saxons for example. So if a question on the Anglo Saxons came up in a SATs test she wouldn't be able to answer it. She would feel a failure. If a question on the history of fashion came up she would be able to answer it and probably no one else would. So, they would feel failures. You can see how ridiculous this can become.

There is a kind of snobbery around having some knowledge instead of other knowledge. And this is what a curriculum can be responsible for if we're not careful.

A National Curriculum sets us up to believe that a child who can answer questions on the subject matter in the curriculum is more intelligent than one who can't, *despite what else they know*, or *even if they know a lot more*.

All subject matter is important. Learning about anything and everything is important. Learning in all areas develops intelligence. There is no one subject that is more important in my view. Knowledge is knowledge whatever the subject. There should be no hierarchy.

The government needs a curriculum. Schools need a curriculum. They use it not only to nationalise the content of what children learn across the country, but also to set standards. And the reason they set standards is because they have to measure and judge. They have to measure and judge performances. They have to measure and judge teachers. And measure and judge schools. But none of this measuring and judging actually helps our children a great deal.

Home educators don't need to do that. You don't need to measure and judge in this way if you don't want to. You don't have to follow the National Curriculum. You don't have to standardise your children's learning. You don't have to follow any kind of curriculum at all if you don't want to and would rather the children's learning were completely independent.

Following the National Curriculum will help to keep parallel to children in school, if you want to do that. It also provides suggestions as to what your children could learn if you don't want to think it up yourself, which can get overwhelming sometimes. But it isn't essential to education. Children can and do learn without a curriculum ever being present. Unfortunately people have been conditioned to think that to learn anything you need a curriculum.

You don't. Learning takes place despite curriculum.

There are all sorts of curricula just as there are all sorts of approaches to learning. A curriculum should be designed to suit the needs of the learner, but the learner's learning should never be enslaved by it. Learner first; then curriculum. If curriculum doesn't suit the learner's needs then it needs changing. There's always the option of no curriculum at all.

Children who are going to take GCSEs or any specific exam will need a specific curriculum to get them there, the exam specification. This is where a specific curriculum designed for a specific outcome has some value. Some families I know didn't use a curriculum until they started on that study yet still gained good grades; their incidental learning up to that point had built the skills and knowledge they needed to tackle them. They then adhered to the specification that would take them to the grades. They did it much quicker than those in schools.

But all learning is valuable whether it takes place within a curriculum or not. Learning that sticks with children the most is the learning that is relevant to them at the time. A curriculum that is national and not personal is least likely to be relevant.

My daughter can punctuate a sentence, use paragraphs, and present a good piece of writing, but she couldn't do that exercise in comma use for the National Curriculum. Did it matter? Is one better than the other?

She didn't do every English exercise in the GCSE English syllabus but she gained herself a place at college without that, on the strength of her initial letter, an interview and top marks for a literacy assessment they asked her to do. So I find it hard to value some of the mundane repetitive exercises the curriculum demands of children earlier in their lives.

What matters is that they have the right skills, knowledge and confidence to do the things they want to do and they may need a curriculum at some point.

But a national one? How can anything that's standardised anticipate what my particular child wants to do with their life?

Your curriculum can be national, natural from the course of your everyday life, personal to the interests of your child, or optional. It's entirely up to you. Working with a curriculum is no guarantee of learning, intelligence or an education, but it may be useful at times. You need not become slaves to it; choose it or lose it, change when you feel like it, make it work for you not the other way round.

Like with all things about education—you can decide.

15

PLOTS, TIMETABLES AND
GIVING CHILDREN CHARGE!

Do you need a timetable? This is another question a bit like the curriculum one and you'll no doubt have guessed what the answer is; you decide.

Also like curriculum, timetables can be a useful tool to help you keep to the plot. But that's all it is, a tool. Not a necessity for learning.

We used many timetables, strategies and plans over our years of home educating and they changed often.

But they did give me some focus at the time. Made me feel there was some direction, process or route we were taking towards an education, rather than us blowing about like a leaf in the wind, as it felt at times. It helped my confidence to occasionally have a plan. And it also seemed that the children liked to have a fixed pattern to follow too—sometimes.

But we mostly didn't use timed-tables. We never managed to stick to them because we never wanted to *time* our learning, it just went on *all* the time.

What usually happened was that we'd stick to them a bit. But soon they became overridden by the more interesting opportunities for learning that arose out of what we were doing.

And I discovered that it was always those more spontaneous activities that resulted in the deepest and most meaningful learning. The most exciting and inspiring of all being those activities the children suddenly had an urge to do themselves. I wasn't going to ruin their motivation by sticking to things we might have written on a timetable. The children had lots of ideas. Timetables just seemed to get in the way.

However, we would talk regularly about how best to plan and organise our days and our activities. The skill of planning and management was a useful one for them to have, but it was mostly done through discussion. I'd chat with the children about it and we'd devise a kind of shortfall list we felt we perhaps ought to cover in a week and the reasons why, for example, that they'd get to experience a range of skills perhaps. It was always talked about.

Even when the children were quite young, when they first came out of school at just six and nine years of age, we talked about their education with them.

We talked about what they might need and want to do. What they'd like to do. We talked about the many fascinating things to know about the world. We talked about what skills they might want in order to gain understanding and knowledge and even more importantly to apply it to life. And the most vital thing of all we talked about with our children was the 'why'.

I always found it fairly impossible to parent my children without giving them the 'why'. Impossible to ask anything of them without giving my reasons for asking.

I admit, when they were little, I did begin to think I might be better off just breathing into a paper bag than giving all these explanations.

But then I remembered how frustrated I felt as a child by having things demanded of me without being given the respect of an explanation. The only reason I ever got was '…because I say so'. It was just not a good enough reason for me. And it still isn't. And that applies to education too.

So, we talked with the children about their education. We'd try and explain how certain skills, which might seem incredibly laborious and dull to them, like writing for example, would be of value to them when they are older. How there was so much wonderful information and recreation available to them if they read. How education and knowledge increases our understanding and leads us towards a better quality of life.

And even though I might have felt like I was hyperventilating at trying to get all these explanations across, it paid off.

The children began to understand something vital. By involving them in the discussion and planning they began to see something about education they did not realise in school.

In school the children thought that education was some mysterious adult-led thing *done to them* by other people, often in unpleasant ways, governed by gruelling timetables and irrelevant strategies.

Once home educating awhile they saw education as something *they could have charge of;* they had power over it and it didn't have to be unpleasant.

They could have as much control over it as everyone else. They could have control over the decision-making. They could have control over the content. Education could be as exciting and as stimulating as they made it. And timetables and strategies were merely tools that were there to enable them to achieve their own goals. Timetables and strategies were not there to enslave them.

In short, we did not *have* to have timetables or strategies to acquire an education, even though we wanted to use them at times. It was useful to have some objectives or plan for the day, especially if we had specific things to do, places to go, people to see. But a timetable is not an education. It is simply a tool. A tool for the children to choose and use.

It was this simple but important concept that had the biggest impact on our children being educated or not. Because once they stopped expecting someone else to push them into education and force timetables on them, once they understood the 'why', they began to take charge of the planning of it themselves. And this is when they begin to truly fly with their education on their own wings, rather than just remain passively sitting and being stuffed with facts.

Taking charge lead them onto all sorts of other valuable personal life-skills: self-motivation, initiative, independence, responsibility, self-confidence, self-assertion and greater personal fulfilment, personal respect and happiness. Alongside knowledge, these are the skills that people need to successfully go forward into living their own lives.

Without these skills people are left open to being victims of whatever life throws at them, which is sadly often the experience of children in schools.

Schools neglect these valuable personal skills in favour of more academic ones. It is having these personal skills that give people power over their lives. Children in school are kept disempowered by never having the opportunity to be truly in charge. They are given trivial responsibilities perhaps, but they are never asked about the fundamentals of their own learning. No wonder so many of them leave unable to make life decisions.

Nothing diminishes the ability to make decisions more than never being given the opportunity to practice doing so—or being *trusted* enough to do so. Children are kept as victims of an education forced upon them by someone else. They are never given charge. Strategies and timetables cleverly mask that fact and are just another structure that keeps adults in charge.

And they also lead parents to misguidedly think that where there's no strategy or timetable, there's no education. Instead of the real truth, that it's the *education* that's important. The strategy or timetable is merely there to facilitate it.

I'm sure that dealing with the children's education in a democratic way, involving them in all plans, encouraging them to make educational decisions, valuing their input, feelings, opinions and integrating these into the perspective of a wider education, is what led them to now being able to organise their time and their lives so well—they learnt the skills by having charge of doing so.

They began to devise their own strategies for being in charge of their own education and what they wanted to accomplish as they grew older. This built the skills they now have to take charge of their own lives.

Timetables, like curriculum, are simply another tool to enable you to organise your time. That's all. Giving children the opportunity to organise their own time and their own learning is a valuable part of their educational development.

16

WHAT ABOUT TERM TIMES, LEARN TIMES AND HOLIDAYS?

It's amazing how we can be so governed by term times.

Even after home educating for a while I could still be influenced by them, even though I knew that education didn't have anything to do with term times at all.

They were usually brought to my attention by the children, and the fact every other family is controlled by them.

'Mu-um?'

Even this one word could make me feel I was about to be manipulated, probably by something I may not like.

'Ye-es?' I'd reply suspiciously.

'Ruth's breaking up from school today; it's end of term.'

'Oh, is it?' I'd feign ignorance knowing full well what was coming.

'Can we break up too?' She'd give a big sheepish grin.

I'd give the usual answer. 'Well, I wasn't aware we had anything to break up from.'

Another grin. 'But can we?'

I'd pause, keeping the suspense and the pretence going a little longer. Then, 'Yeah, go on then, let's.'

And she'd bounce off to go and do the same things she would be doing anyway, 'breaking up' or not.

We'd sometimes go through this little ritual when the schools finished their terms and my children knew their school friends were available for play during the day.

It was partly that, but also because our children did spend some time in school earlier on in their lives and, although freed from it, they still wanted the sense of celebration and release their mates were feeling.

And why not? We all need a change and a celebration. A release from that constant feeling that we perhaps should be doing something more educational than just having fun. It took quite a while for us to get over that idiocy and realise that education just went on all the time, term times, learn times, fun times and holidays.

We educated our children in a mostly autonomous way, with them deciding very much what they worked on, but we'd still motivate them to be busy doing something. We'd encourage them to try new things, make and invent, play actively, be engaged, read, go out, meet others, whatever.

However, although we soon forgot the presence of school terms, it was good for all of us, adults and children in the family, to have a break from all that motivation. To switch off the driving force for a while and stop looking for activities or projects that would stimulate or searching the Internet for active learning sites.

We could drift. We could do things that merely took our fancy and I could stop looking for an educational slant.

So, on one 'end-of-term' occasion, I thought I'd observe what the kids did instead.

The eldest took a heap of books, magazines, sketch book and pens out into the garden, spread herself out on a rug and designed all day, researching her books for inspiration, studying other people's work and incorporating and adapting their ideas into her own.

The youngest decided to build a den out there. This required searching out suitable materials within her environment, putting them together and solving the problem of making the structure strong and upright, in discussion with me or whoever else was available. Then she spent the rest of the day in creative play, making up stories, reading to her toys, imaginative ideas passing through her faster than hot biscuits passed through her mouth.

In other words the children, 'on holiday', covered these skills: reading, research, writing and use of language, drawing and hand-eye coordination skills, problem solving, estimating, analysis, use of materials, investigation, construction, exploration, interpretation, discussion, development of imagination and ideas and creativity. All those skills that teachers had to force reluctant children to practice in schools, usually in a boringly academic and repetitive manner, because the children had been removed from the natural opportunity to practice them anyway.

My children had been busy with all this simply because their minds were freed up from the confines of 'doing education', a trap we sometimes find ourselves falling into how ever autonomous we try and be.

It was a good reminder that we don't always have to be forcing everything in order to further a child's education. And just because there are not set schedules, timetables, term times or regulated practice, it does not mean there will be no learning taking place.

This was proved to me again at the other end of the 'holiday', when school started again. That time when all the other children disappeared off the streets as if the Pied Piper had just been through. When we rejoiced in that wonderful feeling of liberation we had when we were not going back to school with them.

My home educating thoughts took over and I'd realise with panic that it had been ages since we'd done anything that resembled formal education like writing or seen a sum written down. I hadn't motivated them to study anything in particular, they'd mostly been outside and we hadn't produced anything tangible that would impress a LA inspector or the relatives. We'd just drifted. Oh, and been very happy.

So with my awful teacherish hat on I'd persuade them that a bit of writing practice might be worthwhile since they hadn't done any for ages, we'd look at some maths, and we'd discuss things sparked from reading.

And I always got the same surprise.

Even without any kind of formal education what so ever over the last month or so the children had *moved on*. Their writing was neater. Their understanding of maths was greater. Their knowledge was deeper. Their creative work had matured, as had their scientific understanding. *It had all improved.*

It amazed me every time, but it always happened. There was *always* improvement, despite what schools would have you believe about the children missing out when they're absent.

And I believe it happened like this simply because schools overlook an important part of a child's development in their race to educate them for test passing. They overlook the importance of giving *time and personal space* within a child's life for the maturation process.

Just as a child's physical development moves on as time passes, so does their mental growth and capacity for learning and understanding, as long as they are in an environment where they are not inhibited or oppressed, where they are loved and stimulated and paid attention to.

We don't actually need to 'do' education. Or practice a lot. Or force things a lot. Children develop anyway. What we do need to do is allow time for that to happen. Over time they develop mentally and emotionally, essential for developing educationally.

We can't actually force education by continual mundane practice of a narrow batch of skills, but we can put them off if we're not careful.

We can occasionally practice skills, yes. But skills practice alone doesn't make an education. Neither does cramming them full of facts or just teaching them the tricks needed to regurgitate them. None of this is any good without understanding. And that is processed over time. It comes with maturity and personal development, and they need time and space for that.

That's what happened to our children over the summer holiday, whether we'd done anything 'educational' or not.

Education can happen naturally, given time and space. It happens on holiday as much as it happens when we think we're doing something educational. Term times don't actually have anything to do with it.

Except perhaps that's the best time to go away.

17

DEALING WITH OTHERS' RESPONSES

'Not in school today?'

I wish I was paid for every time I had to answer that question when I was out with the children.

People have often asked how I dealt with others' attitudes to our choice to home educate.

At first I thought it was a lovely thing being asked by strangers and I'd say with a little bit of pride; 'No, we're home educators'.

But after a few negative responses in the form of rather weird laughter, a look of disbelief or disapproval, an accusational tone, or an outright 'Well, I don't think that should be allowed,' I became a little more hesitant in explaining.

Another mum, who'd been home schooling for over twenty years and so had begun when it was almost completely unheard of, gave me a little tip. She said that she'd try and gauge the person who asked, whether they asked out of genuine interest or suspicion and pitch her answer to that. Sometimes, when she guessed her response would fall on unsympathetic ears, she'd just answer 'no' and walk off. Some people, she said, prefer not to be enlightened!

It could also be quite soul destroying to witness how people would put the children down. They had occasionally to deal with direct accusations where I was ignored and the children challenged with a question like 'Why aren't you in school?' Although the children would respond politely with 'Because I'm home educated' they could still receive an offensive retort.

Thankfully, this didn't happen often. And as home education has became more widespread over the years the public more often than not are interested and full of admiration. For the children's sake we chatted about why people thought as they did—because home schooling wasn't that well known, because others feared anything that was different, because some folks are just rude—and we talked about what to say, or not. And it was their choice.

But it can be much harder dealing with responses from the nearest and dearest. We had a variety of attitudes from ours ranging from enthusiasm and understanding of our views on schools' failings, through doubt, to complete dismissal.

The problem is, unless people have come across home education first hand, they mostly don't understand it, don't want to understand it, and certainly don't want anyone upsetting their mainstream beliefs. They may also have heard the myths surrounding home schooling, about children running amok, getting taught nothing, not being educated or getting grades, not socialised, and unable to fit in. None of which are true as you and I know.

When people are receptive it's good to explain, help raise awareness and understanding and alter attitudes with the sharing of knowledge. But the family members who are not receptive to alternative approaches can sometimes make you feel you're doing something wrong.

You're not. You're trying to do something better for your child, as thousands of others have successfully done, so you have to keep that at the forefront of your thinking.

The other thing to do is arm yourself with some ammunition.

I'm not talking gunfire here. I'm talking about an armoury of tactics like:

- Your right not to respond
- Accurate information and knowing your subject
- Support from others
- Succinct short responses for tricky moments
- Confidence, courage and faith.

Not responding

Sometimes the best thing really is to say little. What you certainly don't have to do is defend or justify yourself. And it's your right to say 'I don't wish to discuss it here but if you're interested...' With relatives you can ask that they reserve judgement until you're a little way into it. As with all children growing up no one knows how their development or their education will proceed, school children included. Ask for the respect and trust you show to them.

Information

The more you understand how approaches to learning work, how broad and diverse—and successful—they are, the better equipped you will be to offer explanations to people. Research is the key to this, (my other book *Learning Without School: Home Education[1]* may help give you some useful jargon) and there are some brilliant home schooling blogs where families illustrate their day to day lives and how they approach learning. These will help increase your understanding and consequently your ability to talk about it. So, keep reading, surfing and talking to others and building your own knowledge.

Support from others

We all need support. Getting involved with others makes you feel part of a community which can be reassuring after stepping away from the mainstream school-using one. Hearing the way others express their ideas helps you express your own. Talking to others helps formulate your own principles and therefore your ability to talk to non-home schoolers about it. So, connect with other home schooling families regularly and investigate the variety of approaches until you find the right one for you. There is instant support via the Web and this can be immediately comforting, particularly if family members are unsupportive of what you want to do and you can't turn to them when something's bothering you. There are home educating Facebook groups where you can ask others what they do, how they tackle various issues, or just have a rant about your day and get some comfort and reassurance.

Succinct responses

Home educating is such a diverse and wide-ranging approach to learning, as diverse as all the families doing it, that the subject is quite difficult to condense down into short succinct explanations without going into masses of detail. Pick up tips from others on how they do it. Sometimes short responses like the following, to answer the question 'not in school today?' will do in tricky moments out and about;

- We home educate which is a very different and very successful style of learning
- The children are doing all their learning out of school at the present time
- We are too concerned about what goes on in schools so the

children are learning with other home educators for the time being

– We home school—have you come across that before?

– We thought we'd home educate since thousands of others find it so successful

– We home educate. You should look it up, there's masses about it online

– There's so much to learn out of school we thought we'd do it that way for now

Make up some that you feel comfortable with.

Confidence, courage and faith

...are the things it takes in order to home school. So you probably already have them! You just need to keep them to the forefront of your dealings with others and keep them honed through your connections with other home educating families and your developing knowledge and experience. The more knowledge and experience you have, the more your confidence grows. And your courage and faith can be maintained by *remembering the simple truth* (not myth) that there are many, many young people who are now graduated from home educating into college, uni, work, or their own businesses, successfully finding their place in the world. Some of the Home Ed Facebook groups have lists of what they're doing now which make inspirational reading and are perfect ammo for your armoury.

So, have faith that you will get there too. You can hold your head up and be proud of your choice to educate other than in a system that many complain about yet lack the courage to leave in order to practice this successful alternative—as you do.

Its success is already *proven*—you don't need to defend or justify your choice to others if you don't want to.

References
[1] Mountney, Ross. *Learning without School: Home Education*. London: Jessica Kingsley, 2009. Print.

18

No Prizes For Getting There First

Have you ever been on the London Underground?

No doubt those of you who live in London have and I used to when I lived there.

But even though I know what it's like, even though I grew up there and therefore you'd think I was used to it, I am still amazed when I go back. Amazed by the rushing.

Everyone, whatever the time, is always rushing.

You go into the station and everyone's rushing past you on the stairs to get to the platform, even though some of the trains run regularly so if they miss one there'll be another coming along soon. And when you step off the train and leave the station everyone is still rushing. Rushing past you as they head in a rush to the ticket barrier as if it were some kind of race and there's an invisible finishing line they're all desperate to get to.

As everyone rushes past—and we're not exactly dawdling yet we're still being rushed past—and leaves us behind, it does make us feel exactly like that; exactly as if we're being left behind, despite the fact we usually meet them all again seconds later as they stand waiting on the platform.

But with everyone rushing past I start to get anxious. I start to feel like I ought to be rushing too, in case we're missing out on something. What that something might be I have no idea but I definitely feel there must be something I'm missing otherwise why is everybody rushing? Why is everybody surging forward at a stressful pace? What's the point in legging it down the tunnels only to stand waiting because the train's not here yet, fiddling with phones that have no signal?

At first I thought it was just the rush hour. But it seems to happen whatever time of day we go, even coming home again at the end of the day. I appreciate there's far more incentive to rush when one's going home but time of day doesn't seem to make much difference to the rushing even if it makes a difference to the crowds.

And do you know what? It's catching. It's compulsive. Before I know what I'm doing, I'm rushing along too. It's downright unnerving, as infectious as it is stressful. And I really have to get a grip on what I'm doing if I don't want to become contaminated by it. If I want to avoid dashing towards that non-existent finishing line as if I was part of that hypothetical race too. And I have to ask myself the question—do people know there *is no* race, no finishing line and no prizes for getting there first?

I expect the question you're asking right now is what's this all got to do with education? Well, the reason I've described this scenario is because I see exactly the same race happening in education.

Just like me in the underground, it's easy to feel a certain amount of tension and anxiety if we are not all rushing along the same mainline route, towards the same result as everyone else. And not only that, we also tend to feel very, very anxious if we're not doing it at precisely the same time as all the other children, if we don't get off the marks at the same age, reach those imaginary milestones at the same time, and cross that imaginary finishing line at the same stage of maturity.

Whenever I hear parents talk about their child's education, they talk about it exactly as if it were a race and a rush. Certain stages must be gained by a certain time. And if that doesn't happen, like me in the underground, the child will be 'left behind'. In schools this feeling is very real. Heavily unpleasant.

But it doesn't *have* to be like that. And actually there is no 'left behind'. You can achieve anything at any time you want to. And many have.

Education isn't a race. You don't have to achieve in certain time frames. You can actually never stop with education—you can take it as far as you want to, *when* you want to.

There is no point in rushing children along when they're clearly not ready, developmentally, to achieve something. Nothing dire will happen to them if they don't all do the same things at the same time or reach them in the same way.

Another important point to remember is that there is *no finishing line* and there are *no prizes for getting there first*, wherever 'there' may be. There is nothing to be missed out on and the feeling that there maybe is, is simply that—a feeling, not reality. Just like my feeling in the underground.

You have the choice to plan an education that *suits your child's readiness,* which will be far more successful than one you'd pushed them through at an unsuitable pace to 'keep up'. You don't have to pay too much attention to what everyone else is doing. The race everyone else is in needn't concern you. Your child's own particular needs do.

Racing and rushing has nothing to do with education. In fact, spending more time usually gains an education of far higher quality and more meaning than one that has been rushed through in an attempt to meet other people's deadlines that have no personal value to your child.

That is probably part of the reason that we chose to home educate. Because we didn't want our children stressed by the thought that it was a race to get somewhere, or to have them feel stressed if they didn't keep to a particular timeframe.

Time is something we wanted to give them. Time to pay attention to quality and depth of learning rather than experience education as something which, as it rushes on, they must keep up with.

It's best not to let the sight of others racing to this imaginary finishing line, in a mad lemming-like way, distract you from what you believe is right for your children. If rushing and racing isn't right for you, don't get caught up in it.

Just like the folks in the underground, mainstream education can seem a bit lemming-like. I watch families racing towards the eighteen year old bench mark worrying themselves sick about when they'll have to toss themselves off the educational precipice. And I think to myself, do they know there's another way? Do they know that education actually doesn't have to be rushed, doesn't have a time-limit, or a precipice?

Home education provides the opportunity to give children a different educational experience that is not a race. Keep focussed on the way you want to do it; on your children, not mainstream children or systemised education, and move along at a pace that suits your family, where they can fully appreciate the quality and depth of it. Many home educated children I know have achieved what they wanted to achieve, whether qualifications, businesses or work, without sticking to the mainline route or the mainstream timing.

And they did this because they understood that, whether in the underground or in life, even without rushing you will all get where you want to go in the end.

19

CAN LEARNING BE THIS EASY?

I could feel guilty home educating! That was because we always seemed to be having such a nice time and I used to think; education couldn't be this easy surely?

I remember thinking this one day sitting at the table in the kitchen. It was covered with library books, paper, pencils and felt tips. The children were writing and drawing and I was reading them a passage about making paper after the subject had come up the day before. It was quiet. They were listening. And there was a pleasant but industrious peacefulness within the room and within us too.

What a lovely way it was to learn.

Later we cycled the two and a half miles to the playground and shop, getting some exercise and fresh air. We talked about the things we saw on the way, the trees, the species and why we need trees to keep the air clean. They asked questions constantly and we hypothesised and I made a mental note to research it later.

We got home tired, but satisfied. They flopped down to read and look at books and finally watch TV. They seemed full up, content, and happy.

And that was when I used to question. This seemed so natural, so simple, so uncomplicated. Could learning be this easy?

I toyed with this question as I watched our children learn through our years of home educating and I learnt something too. I learnt that most people's perception of education was totally wrong.

Parents have been duped. We have been hoodwinked by politics. We've been over-awed by the enormity of what has become a big educational industry. We have been deceived into believing many things about education that are actually not true.

The first thing we've been conned into believing is that we, us lay-parents, as opposed to the great and the knowledgeable who have been trained to be teachers, are not capable of educating our own children.

Let me put a thought into your mind—teachers are not necessarily any greater or more knowledgeable than you are. You do not have to be mega-bright, mega-knowledgeable or mega-anything to go into teacher training. Believe me; I've done it.

As a training teacher you learn a little about how children learn, as a working teacher you forget that and learn about crowd control, and as you become more experienced you forget any details like the individual and just think about surviving.

There is rarely anything more special about most teachers than there is about the average parent, you included. And the single most important quality a teacher needs to be a good teacher is something that many of them don't have. Something that *you* will have over and above everyone else. That is you *care* about your *individual* child.

As a caring, interested, thoughtful and keen-to-find-out parent you are in a far better position to educate your child than anyone else, teachers included. You don't need specialist knowledge; you just need to have a willingness to find out. You don't need specialist tactics with kids, you just need to be attentive, empathetic and aware. And you don't need to sit and teach them in order to educate them, you just need to be able to encourage them to show interest, to seek and to learn for themselves.

For that's another con—the idea that children always need to be taught in order to learn. They don't.

Children in school are treated like empty receptacles into which teachers cram knowledge by fair means or foul. They have to do this because they have masses of objectives they have to force kids to meet for the purpose of measurement, of both the kids and the school, and they have a time restraint on which to do it.

That is just one way of educating. Often an unsuccessful and harmful way.

There are other ways. Ways where you don't have to cram your kids with irrelevant information—you choose the information (the curriculum) and you choose the time you want to take to do it. Yet even if you don't have a timetable or curriculum children still become educated.

Curricula, syllabi and time restraints have complicated education. Schools have an agenda they have to meet. They have a National Curriculum of subjects and they have a set time to deliver it. They have to fill kids' heads with lots of information and then get them to regurgitate it in order to pass tests and take exams, irrespective of whether it is understood. That's what schools do. That's what they've made education into.

But that's their sort of education, if indeed you could call it that. And that is only one narrow way of achieving it.

Everyone has a different way of learning. Schools and teachers do not have the time to accommodate all the different ways individuals have of learning. But home educators can.

When you home educate you can choose whatever you want to learn, whatever interests or is relevant, and the way in which you want to learn it. And this makes it easier, rather than more complicated, because when you are learning things you want to learn, rather than things someone else deems you should learn, then you learn it more effectively.

You can set yourself targets based on what you want to achieve and you can decide how best to reach your targets. This makes it all relevant, and as such a more pleasant and meaningful process. Education becomes a personal process relevant to the individual, not a cramming of irrelevant information. Teaching doesn't necessarily come into it.

Many home educators I know do not really teach. They encourage their children to be interested in a whole range of subjects. They facilitate the learning of them by support. They show their kids where to find information, ways of researching, ways of recording, ways of taking it in. They show them how they might want to work towards exams and how they might achieve results. Most importantly which exams are relevant and that vast quantities of tests and qualifications are not.

So, learning and education can have a whole new outlook. One that can be easy, fascinating, unlimited to curriculum and one that belongs to you rather than to a school. Learning is a very personal thing. Home education keeps it that way. To have this kind of education you do not need to have an outside teacher, you do not need a curriculum decided by anyone else. And you do not need to be tested.

Testing being another ritual we've been duped into believing has value.

Testing in schools is necessary to prove something to somebody. That is all. It has little—if any—educational value in itself, or to the child. It actually isn't necessary to learning at all. Ask yourself; what do tests do? Do they teach my child anything new?

Testing throughout all those years does more harm than good. Children don't need it. Being tested is no guarantee of learning. Test passes do not equal intelligence. And anyone can be educated without ever having passed a test. That's a truth—not a con.

82

Sometimes I feel that schools, teachers, curricula and testing complicate something which is actually quite simple. Learning is as simple as having an interested learner who is keen to learn and someone who wants to help them. That's you!

To be a home educator you have to like being with your children. You have to be interested in learning and growing, but you probably already are or you wouldn't be reading this. And you have to be committed and believe in what you're doing, even though you may not yet have all the answers. No one has all the answers. Having the answers isn't important. Knowing you haven't and thinking about it is.

I would be oversimplifying it to say home educating was dead easy. But I wanted to clear a few of the more irrelevant complications that institutionalised education has placed upon our paths.

Equally, it would be oversimplifying it to say that parenting is dead easy too. We all know it isn't. But we all manage our parenting, don't we?

Home education is more about management skills than teaching skills. It is more about caring and encouraging than delivering a lesson. It's about igniting passion and curiosity, not quelling it with an irrelevant curriculum. And it is more about continued personal growth than it is about testing what has already grown.

That's the best thing I learnt through home educating; learning really can be that easy!

20

WHAT ABOUT PROVING IT TO THE LA?

You'll be very busy as a home educating family, naturally. The trouble is you could end up being less busy being engaged in any valuable learning and more busy trying to create and find proof of it.

For these are two different things were talking about here—a) really educating, and b) proving it to someone else. Most pressingly (after the relatives), proving it to the Local Authority. You can waste an awful lot of time over it, like I did in the 'Science' story.

Let's think about schools for a moment, because it helps to understand what really happens rather than what we think is happening. Schools have to spend masses of time proving that they're educating children. They have to provide proof for parents, for governors, for inspectors, for the government. They have the worrying prospect of Ofsted inspections hanging over them.

Ofsted is supposed to inspect, regulate and, consequently, improve the education in schools. But many teachers and heads are now saying that it doesn't work, for all manner of reasons, one of which is that it disrupts inspirational teaching and forces unnatural coercion into the learning process. The Guardian website[1] has regular postings from professionals under their 'Secret Teacher' section which often bemoan this.

In this way schools are trapped. They have to keep on with this dogged process of providing records and ticking sheets. Children have to do the same. Teachers have to do extensive and time-consuming form filling. Head teachers are swimming in it. And while all this is being coped with, the time and energy for new and inspiring learning experiences is dwindling away.

The big fallacy is, though most people fail to see it, that recording what's been covered in a lesson is no guarantee it's been learnt. For example; just as I might have a pudding to prove I've done some baking, it doesn't mean I've learnt how to do it again.

So, for a child to be perpetually recording things they've covered is not always going to be valid. Sometimes writing down something newly learnt helps reinforce the learning. But not always. And it uses up time that could be spent in more inspiring ways. It's something many teachers also say they regret spending time on, but their hands are tied.

When you're home educating, this style of record keeping is not necessarily something you always have to do unless you want to and it's relevant. But home educating families certainly don't *have* to get into that laborious practice for fear that they're not doing what schools do and worry they are therefore not providing a good education. That *won't be the case*.

Besides, I've known school children who can produce books of stuff they've covered in a term but ask them about it and they've forgotten. I know teachers who groan under the weight of the record keeping they have to do and groan most particularly about the fact that it is hardly ever referred to. And I've heard head teachers say they've kept extensive records of children's progress through Primary school which have been ignored at Secondary.

So, the business of providing proof of an education can disrupt other valuable things which could be going on. This is where home educators can strike their own balance. A balance between serving children's educational needs and feeling confident about that when we're contacted by our LA, as this is an aspect many worry about.

To do that my advice would be to:

a) Be clear about what the LA is allowed, or not allowed to do in terms of their interaction with your children, and what *you* want to happen— *or not*.

b) Find easy ways of recording all the things you do with your children so that you can talk about it confidently with the LA when you need to.

In respect of a) an excellent resource is the website Ed Yourself [2]. On the FAQs page it tells you what the authority is allowed to do and, just as importantly, what it's *not* allowed to do. For example, you do not *have* to supply written evidence of provision, so wasting your child's time making them write stuff or fill in workbooks just for this purpose is not necessary. It might be part of your provision for other reasons, but it's reassuring to know that *how* we demonstrate our provision doesn't necessarily mean masses of written stuff to show. Your contact from the LA should not take the form of an inspection and you are not obliged to endure anything like the Ofsted process. The website has regular updates about how home educators and Local Authorities are building better understanding of their respective roles.

It is also useful to connect with other home educators and networks in your area for exact up-to-date information from others who've had contact with their authority. Talking with others also helps you develop clear ideas about your home education approaches, how and what you want to provide (this can be anything from a school-style structured approach to completely autonomous learning). This will give you confidence when talking to the LA. Some home education communities offer a mentor or friend who could be in attendance too. You can also find out what to expect from your own LA from their particular website via the government services website[3]—search for 'home education'.

In respect of b), some parents find, for their own reassurance, that it's helpful to keep a record of their activities as much for them to remember just how much they've done, and be able to talk about it, as anything. They do this in a variety of ways; jottings in a dairy, keeping a box of the children's work/books/paraphernalia etc, photographs of activities or completed projects, online blogs or memos, whatever works and can be updated easily. In these records it's also possible to note all the incidental learning, conversations, trips, etc which are so valuable. When you build notes of your activities you'll be amazed how much you've achieved. And this helps build confidence in what you're doing.

However, do try not to let this need to keep a record corrupt your valuable home educating days. Real education lies in the *experience for the child* itself *not* in the recording of it.

The more you home educate the more you think about education, the more you talk to other home educators, then the more you will be able to refine your understanding of what you think education really is and be able to talk about it to others like LA staff.

If we concentrate on the real business of educating our children, it is bound to be evident in our conversation and we are better equipped to stand our ground when others may doubt us, LAs included.

But it's so important to remember that there is much more educative value in the experience you are giving your children than in providing proof of it.

References

[1] www.theguardian.com
[2] www.edyourself.org
[3] www.gov.uk

21

Is It Enough That They Don't Like School?

We got asked a lot of questions as we home educated. Either that or the subject got avoided like an unmentionable personal odour.

Most of the questions were from genuine interest. Things like; do you have to be a teacher? Do you do tests? Do you have to follow the National Curriculum? Do they follow a timetable? Do you have a schoolroom?

All the answers to which were an easy 'no'.

But one of the questions I found the hardest to answer was 'Why don't they go to school?'

This was because I knew the answer I wanted to give wasn't the one folks were looking for. It was too easy. Too simplistic. And definitely not academic or educational enough.

My simple answer was 'Because they don't like it.' But to others this didn't seem a good enough one.

However, this was the fundamental reason and good enough for us simply because it affects everything. If they don't like school they won't get the best out of it. If they feel unhappy they won't learn or, even worse, they'll be put off learning completely. If they are uncomfortable in that environment they are not going to take anything on board or reach their potential. And if they are stressed then they are only going to get ill.

Our children's unhappiness, unrest, boredom, disinterest, stress and illness were all as a result of not liking school and were good enough reasons in my mind for us to try something else.

Of course, 'because they don't like it' is the short answer. The longer answer is to do with respect.

Why is it that just because children are children we dismiss so readily their right to have their wishes respected? We do not *value* their likes and dislikes, and often disregard them, thinking we know better.

I don't know about you but it would infuriate me to be told that I didn't know whether I liked sprouts or not. Or stock car racing. Or parties. Or big crowds. Or traffic jams. I would find it a huge insult to have my likes and dislikes treated as if they were of no consequence at all, just because bigger, older people said they knew what I liked and disliked better than me.

Now I know there are times when we can be wrong about what we like and dislike. I was wrong for a lot of years about sprouts. Or was I? Was it just that a part of me went through a change and got to like sprouts better? Perhaps.

Sometimes we change, sometimes we don't. Sometimes we have other diverse or subconscious reasons for not liking something. And always we have deep down fears.

But I think we're mostly accurate about what is right for us at the time. At the time, I didn't like sprouts. So what? Now I do. Big deal! I know it's always important to try things and I do try things. I kept giving sprouts a go.

But however much I try—and I do still try occasionally—I just don't like crowded places and school was a crowded place. Even now, years and years later, I still don't like crowded places. And I think crowded places are going to be one of the things, even though I'm open to change, that I am never going to enjoy. It's just me.

Crowds were just one small part of school I didn't like. And even when I walk into schools now, just as when I walked in as a child, a student, a teacher and a parent, I still don't like schools. That's just the way I am.

But when I was little that feeling was never respected. Yet I was expected to respect others' opinions, without them respecting mine. I was supposed to accept that I didn't know what I liked. I was expected to believe that there was something *wrong* with me because I had this dislike and it wasn't normal because others didn't have it.

I think it is a good enough reason that our children didn't like school. Enough of a reason to change things for them. For we respect their opinions. We respect their knowledge of their own minds. They gave school a fair trial. We discussed their reasons behind their likes and dislikes. We discussed various issues with school, including the benefits. I never told them I disliked school—ever—as I didn't want to influence them.

The issues they had with school were different from mine and different

88

for each of them, quite individual. It was a collection of things; the hubbub for one; unfriendly relationships; lack of respect shown to them; the boring pointlessness of the work they had to do; the irrelevance of it; the bullying; the atmosphere; the behaviour of some of the teachers... the list went on and on. Most of it was to do with personal respect.

But it culminated in the fact that they didn't like it. It made them unhappy. It made them lose their smiles. It eventually made them ill, sad little people. So not liking school was a good enough reason for ours not to go. It wasn't the reason itself, it was the implications. Many people couldn't see them.

I felt many adults cringe in response when I told them. I sensed them bristle with the need to tell me that I shouldn't pander to their every whim. I can assure you I didn't. Ask the children!

And I had people say to me in a snooty way, 'Well, I don't like work but I have to go', which is, of course, true except most adults seem to overlook the glaring obvious difference; they have *choices*. Choices to alter their work. Choices to alter their conditions. Choices about how they are treated and how they respond. Choices that children *don't* have. In school, children are powerless.

The attitude that children should go to school whether they like it or not, as a good preparation for adult life, is bizarre; it is nothing like adult life.

Never in your adult life will you encounter anything like school.

And if people think that adult life is a grind so children should go to school to get used to this adult grind, then perhaps instead they should change their adult life.

As adults we always have opportunity for choice and change, although many people don't exercise this choice. And adults can mostly put themselves in positions where their feelings and preferences are respected.

Admittedly we all need guidance and perspective at times. Adults and children alike. But children have likes and dislikes as much as adults do and they have good reasons for them. Take my friend's child who, as an infant, just wouldn't eat bread. Mum thought she just didn't like it and kept encouraging her. Turns out she had a life threatening allergy to gluten. There was a reason for her dislike.

There are good reasons why our children don't like school. When was the last time you endured it day after day, year after year? Would you like it? And are your feelings something that should be disregarded because someone else knows better? Or would you like them to be respected?

Just because children are small doesn't justify a total disrespect of their feelings. We don't always know better. In fact, I sometimes question whether we know better at all.

So, when I was asked why my children didn't go to school I sometimes gave people the long answer. And sometimes I deliberately and facetiously said it was because they didn't like it. Then I did a runner.

For I learnt too, that my dislikes were valid. And I knew I was going to dislike some people the minute they screwed up their face at my reply!

22

Losing Contol!

For me, sibling conflict is one of the most wearing things we have to deal with as parents. Add home education into it, with the children being at home and together all the time, and it can be very challenging when kids fall out.

It stressed me out, churned my stomach, and could make me lose control especially when I got involved.

But then I found that getting involved actually tended to make it a whole lot worse.

Not getting involved was as hard as having chocolate in the house and not eating it. Very tricky! But there's no doubt that the less fuss I made of their conflicts the better it was for everyone. Better for me because getting involved was going to mean being torn in two and inevitably raising my blood pressure. And better for them, as the last thing they needed was another shrieking and irrational participant to fan the flames.

But another reason I tried not to get involved was because I wanted to leave it up to them to sort out. To begin to take responsibility for themselves.

Children have to be able to close these disputes. To be able to take themselves forward from being stuck in a bog of conflict, to be able to compromise, deal with unpleasant feelings associated with not getting their own way, and see that there are ways of living together satisfactorily even when they don't get their own way.

If they could do that themselves as they matured, rather than have me sort it out for them, then they would have a valuable life skill for their future.

Now, there's no way a small infant can do this. Children have to be at a certain stage before they can understand the idea of non-ego-led behaviour and be able to see beyond always getting their own way and having control over others. Because that's what most disputes are about

—someone wanting control over someone else.

And, if I'm honest, that's probably the only reason I wanted to get involved; because I wanted control too.

Wanting control is usually why kids fall out. And that's why I often fell out with them. That's probably why all parents fall out with their kids. Simply over control issues.

Parents want kids to do things the kids don't want to do. Or kids want to do things their parents don't want them to do. Or kids want control over their siblings. Or children want their parents to do things they don't want to. And we all have valid reasons.

But often, if we're brutally honest about our adult reasons for requiring things of our children, they're as much about us wanting our own way as anything.

Obviously there are always health, safety and sanity issues. But I think many of us actually use those issues as an excuse just to have that bit of extra control. Just to make our lives easier. And we sometimes use education as an excuse too, just as schools do.

Schools, and some parents, sometimes use education as a way of keeping control over children. Keeping them busy. Keeping their heads down at academic things. Keeping them from doing things that are messy, noisy, challenging or demanding just because it's a bother. We can even keep them occupied with things that look educational but which actually have little value. So-called 'educational' games often fit this description, even if there are some genuinely valuable ones.

Education is also used for control in the form of a dire threat, such as 'Do your writing or you'll never get anywhere in life'. A statement that is just not true.

Children in school have the minimum amount of say (if any) in the activities they do. They must feel so completely at the mercy of everyone else and there's nothing worse than that for making you feel angry and frustrated. It's no wonder some of today's teenagers do some of the things they do.

Obviously, some characters like to be controlled. Like to have others lead the way. That's part of some peoples' make-up. But I would guess many don't. And it's no wonder that trouble arises, that children vent these feelings of pent-up frustration on whoever's available and the easiest to bully.

With the pressures of control from parents, teachers, schools, an over prescriptive education and a system of exams that threatens children with a written-off life should they fail them, it's no wonder children crumple under it all.

As home educators perhaps we can relinquish some of this control and dissipate some of these frustrations.

I'm not saying we shouldn't care for, attend to, or have input into our children's lives. What I'm trying to say is, that under the guise of caring for and educating them, we perhaps don't need to have as much control as we think we do. Either in sorting out their disputes, trying to keep everyone sweet, or even over the content of their education. We can hand over the control of it to them sometimes. We can give them a bit more choice—a lot more choice.

Of course, this isn't the easiest option for us parents. It may seem incredibly scary. It takes a huge step of faith, a lot of discussion, interaction and guidance, much explaining about behaviour and learning and an enormous amount of patience.

But, in the end, I think children do take charge of themselves and their education. They do not need us to have control all the time. However, they will never take charge of themselves if someone else always has control over them.

I also believe that most children are intelligent enough to understand that sometimes parents have good reasons for wanting them to do what we ask of them. That is *if* we do have good reasons and don't just want our way because it's easier.

Equally, children also have good reasons for wanting to do what they do. Harmful behaviour is never acceptable but as long as they feel listened to, have opportunities to express their feelings and have their say over their own activities, they are then more willing to compromise and to allow others to be in control of them when appropriate. But control for control's sake is not appropriate.

It helps sometimes for us to ask ourselves the real reasons for our actions. To relinquish some of our control over our children and gradually teach them to take responsibility for their actions and their learning. It's an important aspect of their education.

23

THERE'S NOTHING WRONG
WITH OUR CHILDREN

I want to reassure you all of something: there's nothing wrong with your children.

I say this because there are folks who would make out that there is. They make out that there must be something wrong with a child who doesn't thrive in school, for example, or doesn't read easily, or can't run as fast as others, or who is shy.

It's just that people like to make out that others who are not the same as them must have something wrong with them. But the real truth is that *everyone is different*.

It took a while for this to really sink in with me, particularly the implications.

Take gardening as an example. I just never took to it, my plants seemed to die when everyone else's flourished. There must be something wrong with me, surely, for this to happen.

I did try. My mother was a great gardener. Her roses yielded abundant blooms, her cuttings thrived, her shrubs grew enormous.

Mine didn't.

All mine did was wither. I planted plants she bought me and they died. I even managed to kill houseplants. I'm sure all I ever did was look at them and they shrivelled.

This soon led me to believe there definitely must be something wrong with me.

I'd watch my mother in raptures round the garden centre and I'd look at my watch and think, 'How much longer?' I'd listen to my friends going on about their plants and their gardens and I'd feel there must be a gaping hole in my emotional development because I just couldn't feel what they did. I used to visit my friend who had a creeping fig right over her living room ceiling, yet all my attempts at growing one had failed. I was useless.

It took a while for this to change.

Firstly, I do actually like gardening now. It's something I've grown into, pardon the pun. Now that I have a little more time I enjoy it more. Now, also, that I have had time to mature my skills and accept that a slower turnover of success is just as fulfilling as a quick fix.

So I began to feel a little better, a little less like I'd got this major inability.

I also learnt two important things; however hard I might have tried at the time I just wasn't ready for the delights of gardening. I just couldn't apply myself enough to hone the necessary skills and patience. And I don't think that whatever I did, at that time, I could have made any difference.

But, secondly, there was nothing wrong with me because of that. It wasn't an inability, a learning difficulty, or anything else you want to call it. It was just the way it was and I shouldn't sweat it.

So, what about the skills that are pressed on kids in the form of their education? Isn't it the same thing?

The way I see it, many, many skills are pressed on kids as a means to educate them. Knowledge is forced into them. Subjects are heaped upon them. Achievements are expected from them. None of which children particularly choose. Few of which they particularly like. Even fewer bearing any relation to the children's lives at all.

And then schools make out there's something wrong with those kids who don't achieve.

Yet I can't see the difference between this and the gardening really. It seems the same problem to me. It seems we expect children to acquire the skills *we* think they need, regardless of whether *they* think they need them, and then suggest there's something wrong with them when they don't succeed. Isn't that a bit bizarre?

A love of gardening was something I matured into. I acquired the skills to do it when I became ready. There was nothing wrong with me before I was ready, or before I had those skills.

Many of the things we ask children to do by way of education they are simply not ready for, or able to do, or interested in. But it doesn't mean there is anything *wrong* with our children. That's just the way children are.

I find it quite *extraordinary* that we set a curriculum of subjects that are as important to children as rheumatism and then expect them to enjoy studying them.

We set them tasks to do that are as appealing to them as cleaning out toilets is to me and expect them to do them willingly.

We expect them to practice skills that are as irrelevant to them at that stage in their lives as training to be an astronaut is to me as a parent.

And then, when they don't succeed (surprise, surprise!) we call them failures. We make out there's something wrong with them. Extraordinary!

It takes a long time to mature into things. Like wine and good cheese, Shakespeare and advanced maths. And some of us never do. But that's okay. There's nothing wrong in that. There are other nutritious things besides wine and cheese to enjoy, other subjects to get to grips with. We have to be at a certain stage to see the benefits of certain tasks (like cleaning the toilets, or writing perhaps). And some may never reach enjoyment of them. (Definitely me with the toilets). But there's *nothing wrong* in that either. Some skills will never, ever be for us, however hard we push and practise. It's just the way we are—it's called individualism. There'll be other skills we're good at.

Just because your child can't write, or can't read, can't do maths, doesn't take to sitting down doing any kind of school work, or didn't thrive or achieve in school, *does not mean that there is anything wrong with them*. We must make sure we avoid thinking about our children in that way.

What we must do is *allow* each individual to be the way they are without thinking there's something wrong with them if they're not the same as other children.

Some kids mature into reading late. Some kids mature into writing late. Some take ages to understand the intricacies of maths. Some take ages to understand the value of doing things they can't see any immediate relevance to. Some kids never get it at all. Some kids have very special other skills that are harder for us to appreciate and value. It doesn't make them wrong for being like that. Some dyslexic children have very special skills that those of us who are not dyslexic will never have but it doesn't make anyone wrong.

One skill is not more valuable than the other, even though advocates of the National Curriculum would have us believe otherwise. It's hard in our current educational climate to keep faith. To value all the diverse things our children can do rather than only notice what they can't. It is hard to truly believe in our wonderfully individual children and the special talents they have, particularly when those talents don't match those required to succeed in schools.

But if we want our children to grow with confidence—and confidence is the very best tool they can have—if we want our children to succeed in life, we must never begin to act as if there's something wrong with them when they don't achieve the same as others. They will achieve other things that are equally as valuable to them. We must support them for who they are and what they *can* do.

I hear stories of children having to see an educational psychologist because they're not achieving at school. That to me is the same thing as dragging me to see an educational psychologist just because I couldn't achieve at gardening.

I didn't need to see an educational psychologist; I needed to do something different.

I appreciate there are rare and specific problems, but generally children don't need to see an educational psychologist either; they need to do something different. They need a different kind of education. That's all. There's nothing else wrong.

I know adults who can't drive and have never managed to learn. I don't tell them they need to see an educational psychologist because of it.

Everyone is different. Each child has different learning strengths. We don't need to change the children, we need to change our attitude. It's only when we try and make everyone the same that problems arise.

No, there is *nothing wrong* with our children. Nothing wrong if they don't fit in school. Nothing wrong if they don't like academic stuff. Nothing wrong if they take a long time maturing into certain skills. And we must guard against being talked into believing that there is.

24

THE OUTDOOR MIRACLE

I have a little miracle that I want to share with you.

I've often mentioned it before but in case you missed it I thought it was worth including here. Because it's so simple, it's so overlooked, and it's so helpful for those days when you're all driving each other mad, which happens in *all* households not just home educating ones, so don't worry it's not just you.

It came to me one Wednesday. We'd been cloistered in the house since the weekend. Moods were low. Irritation was high. And I wondered whether I should risk it?

It wasn't often we got that housebound. We were most likely to have been off somewhere, at some point, seeing people or taking a trip to the swimming pool or library. In fact, it was more often the case that we had to actually book time to stay at home and achieve things.

But this particular week worked out different and I suddenly found 'The Mood' had set in. This was when we all argued with each other over the silliest things. I mean, I couldn't care less whether the cornflakes were stale, how they got stale, or whose fault it was, but you know how it goes...

That was when I wondered if I should mention it.

When the youngest started irritating the cat, yet again, and the teenager started irritating the youngest, yet again, and I started irritating them both, yet again, I decided to pluck up courage and say,

'Come on – we'll go for a walk.'

G – r – o – a – n!

The body language of my teenager couldn't have been clearer if she'd shrieked the words 'Are you mad?' at me. The youngest had a more logical brain and concocted a recipe of excuses.

'My favourite programme's on in a minute.' (Isn't that always the case?)

98

'Teddy doesn't want to!' 'I'm too tired.' 'My little finger hurts.'

'Well, never mind darling, you can walk on your feet instead of your little finger.' I tried to cajole, but it didn't work at raising a smile.

'But it's wet and muddy, my jeans will get dirty. Why can't we go out on a nice day?' groaned the teenager, ever conscious of her outfit. I was thinking that by the time she'd changed her outfit, as she'll no doubt have to do, the season will have turned anyway but that was just my silent sarcasm.

Youngest clutched teddy and looked reproachfully at me over his head. I tried to not let this barrage of resistance get me down and gathered coats.

'Come on, teddy can come too. I'll make him a sling,' I said. Seeing I was winning with her I tried another tack with the teenager.

'You know how much the exercise does you good. And it's wonderful for your complexion!'

She groaned again, but rolled off the settee to go and get changed. We got teddy in the right position; this took two attempts as I put him so he couldn't see out first off—I should have known better.

While we stood waiting for teen to decide what to wear, with me trying to keep the enthusiasm going, I began to waver and thought, 'Why do I bother?'

Then we got outside, got going and I remembered why; the miracle happened.

Within five minutes the teenager, who was walking at a suitable distance from an annoyingly right parent, was singing. Yes—singing. Yes—the one who'd been moaning before! The youngest was skipping along, forgetting her tiredness and her little finger.

Within ten minutes the teenager was chatting to me happily about all the things in life she'd got to look forward to and how great everything was. She was smiling and rosy. The youngest was chatting happily to teddy, telling him all about everything she could see, just like I'd done for her.

Within fifteen minutes everyone was laughing and happy and joking with one another, me included, and there was absolutely no sign of 'The Mood'!

It happened almost every time. It was my antidote to the indoor doldrums. We just needed to *get outside*.

It is so easy in our culture of comfort and convenience, safety and easy indoor entertainment to forget one of our basic human needs. And that's the need to be outdoors, under the sky.

Sunshine and daylight are recognised treatments for the condition Seasonally Affective Disorder, where sufferers become depressed if not getting enough time under natural light. But that aside, I believe we all, particularly children, become moody and irritable if we are cloistered inside for too long. We all have a need for regular doses of daylight, movement, fresh air and outdoor space. Although many are reluctant to acknowledge the fact, especially if the weather's not that inviting. If steady exercise is included the benefits double.

It doesn't really matter whether you are in the country or in the city; it still seems to work the same.

We lived in an environment where we were surrounded by wide-open spaces. But when we spent time in the city I still noticed the same lift in our moods as soon as we stepped out onto the street—after all, it is still under the same sky. Even a brisk walk along the pavement changed the mood dramatically. And most cities have accessible places to take children to let off steam.

Which was all that was needed. For me too. I wasn't too proud to run and skip if the need took me, despite the children groaning with embarrassment.

I think of all those children shut in schools for hours on end who never get a decent amount of time outside. I think of our culture's indoor, gaming, social media and online lifestyles. And I think; is it any wonder that so many people have such long faces, low moods and pent-up emotions? Such a shame when there's such a simple antidote.

When we got back, the outfit got changed back again and the teenager flopped back down with her book on the settee once more, the youngest sat with Ted in front of the television. But they had roses in their cheeks, contentment on their faces, and no one was irritating anybody.

That's my miracle. You should try it too!

25

EDUCATION IS NOT TIDY

I'm sure there were many who thought we were such an untidy family.

Our house was always strewn with the debris of home education. There were bits and bobs everywhere. Books, paper, card, boxes of pens, glue, empty sticky-tape rolls, scissors, snippets of stuff and mountains of less-identifiable things used for experimenting, making and constructing. There were toys, building kits, craft kits and magazines. And even the dishes might be dumped on the side neglected because something interesting crawled up the window and we had to stop and investigate it.

But then, we were a home educating family. And home educating isn't necessarily tidy. In fact, I would go as far as to say that most education, true education as in learning about all the wonderful things in life and experiencing them first hand as you often need to do to become truly educated, is not tidy either.

A school style education has conned us that it should be. Like the one the government produces for us and implements via a National Curriculum. One which follows a specific pre-determined route towards a particular outcome dictated by someone other than the learner, designed by those in education who profess to know about such things. There are tidy courses in books which take a learner along a well cut path through what appears to be a jungle of things one apparently needs to know in order to have a successful life. And these pathways can be reassuring and useful. They can provide a confident trail through territory most of us haven't encountered before. A trail that is so well trodden and tested its outcome is supposed to be certain. (Questionable!)

But that is only one sort of route. And it is not the *only* one that will lead to an education, well trodden, tested and tidy though it may be. And not one we always have to follow.

I was never one to follow a pre-destined pathway without trying alternatives. And I suspect I'm like many in that I'm not afraid of untidy and I like the appeal of venturing off the path into the jungle sometimes.

Education is a bit like a jungle. A massive, blooming, abundant jungle. There are explorations, investigations and experiments to do, things to discover, information to unveil, personal development to be made and skills to acquire. None of which need be predetermined, but all of which provide as equally a valuable learning experience as a neat academic one, even though it looks untidy from the outside.

But here's an important point; *education is not only valuable if it is tidy*. Nor is it less valuable if it is not prescribed, or doesn't have set objectives, or doesn't follow a structured path, or come in a graded package. For learning goes on all the time whether it is packaged or not.

Every experience teaches us. Some of the more profound experiences that we have teach us things that are life-changing.

Even the smallest experiences teach something. Each small experience your child has he will learn from. Even his experiences in play, in fact, mostly his experiences in play, particularly the experimental, explorative or imaginative kind. You know—the really untidy stuff.

All these untidy, unstructured experiences all fit together in the end to make an education. Education doesn't always require you to start at a specific point or end at a specific point. Following a prescribed curriculum doesn't really matter. It's the *experiences* that matter the most; the *experience of learning*.

For example; tidy courses in history take the learner chronologically through Early Man, all the Ages, the Romans etc, all the kings and queens and politics. And quite often you are not expected to move forward until one bit is learned. And, once covered, that topic is unlikely to be returned to.

Yet there's no guarantee that learning is going to be cemented in a child's mind that way rather than if you just untidily dip into periods of history when they're relevant, when an interest sparks or when a programme comes on the telly.

Untidy this may be, but in the end a picture of history will come together. In fact, if these less structured experiences of history are more *meaningful, fun and relevant* to the child's life at the time, if it was something that sparked an interest at that particular moment like a visit to a transport museum for example, then it is more likely to be learned than studying rote fashion from a course book just for the sake of it. Our brain just sorts it all out and pieces it all together like a logical microchip. We don't always have to be orderly.

I'm not saying that we should never follow a tidy course to a specific outcome. That way of doing things is valuable too at times.

What I am saying is that it helps to remember that all the untidy learning that takes place outside of that is *equally* valuable. More so if it is relevant to the child.

Educating in this untidy spontaneous way might not feel familiar. But have faith. It is just as valuable a journey as any other.

For education, as well as being untidy sometimes, *is a journey.* A journey of development, not the rote learning of set outcomes. It is a journey that pulls together various learning experiences along the way. It is a journey that never has to end. A continuing, life-long, exciting adventure. You will miss so much if you stick to tidy. Experiential learning never happens on cue, yet so often these are the lessons that stay with us.

And another thing about untidy is that it *stimulates.* Stimulated children are learning children. There needs to be stuff around to stimulate and arouse interest. Untidy means there are activities going on. And remember; what we adults reckon is untidy is usually a fascinating opportunity for adventure and discovery to a child.

When I walk into an untidy house (yes, there are others besides mine), I am immediately stimulated by the things going on there. I'm not talking about last week's washing up or the mouldy apple core under the settee. I'm not talking slovenly. I'm talking about lives being lived. People doing things. Stuff going on. Lives with things going on in them are lives where learning is going on.

When I walk into an immaculately sterile show home part of me switches off. The kids do too. There's nothing to stimulate them there.

This way of educating is very different from the type of learning that everyone's used to seeing in school. But different isn't wrong. Don't worry if it seems to be untidy, disjointed or totally messes up the house. If the things you get up to make your house untidy, you can be absolutely sure that there is learning going on, that someone in that house is alive and active, busy, living a life and becoming educated as a result.

Education can sometimes be untidy, experiences usually are. But remember; *experience equals education.* And it's often the untidiest sorts that educate the best.

26

WHY GETTING IT WRONG IS RIGHT

Home educating is brilliant! When it goes well, that is. When the day runs smoothly, when there's no shouting, conflict, name calling, frustration—not even from the children!

Only joking—it was brilliant most of the time really and when it wasn't I consoled myself with the fact that nothing can be brilliant all the time. Parents with children in school will have just as many challenges and wobbles; family life has many challenges and wobbly bits, it's not just home education that creates them. Even the bad days can show us the right way forward sometimes.

Some of the best times were seeing the children absorbed with things they'd chosen to do, stretching their minds and increasing their skills, times that fell into place for them instead of falling apart.

When I saw them suddenly able to do things they otherwise couldn't, it was amazing; it was me that got to see it, not some stranger in a school who'd probably miss it as they had thirty others to attend to. When I saw the children using skills that I thought they'd never attain, or reach an understanding that at one point seemed impossible, it was brilliant.

I could always tell when it was working well because it was a moment when they were independently busy; not requiring my assistance or even my attention. They were just so totally absorbed—I didn't exist. For a moment anyway.

And moments like that I used to stand back, making a concerted effort not to interfere, and ask myself how it had arrived.

Was it because I taught them well? Was it because I knew some magic parenting strategies? Was it because I'd given them lessons in studying? Or perhaps it was because they were just such contented and motivated children? I wish…!

No. It was none of those things, I decided. It was nothing to do with lessons, strategies, or anything I might have got right.

I came to the conclusion that it was simply because they'd had the opportunity, without any shame attached, to do things *wrong*.

Now that may sound appalling to you. No one, in their right mind, ever gets anywhere doing things wrong, do they?

Consider this:

My first child was in school for four years. Being a sensitive and conscientious child she absorbed the hidden messages that for any of her work to be worthwhile in anybody's eyes it had to be *correct*. It had to be done in a certain way. It had to be produced in the way the teacher approved of. It had to meet all the requirements laid down in the prescribed curriculum.

Now, conscientious or not, any child would soon sense this kind of pressure to do things *right*, and there is an enormous amount of pressure in schools to do just that, to work towards one particular outcome. And pressure is exactly what she felt.

She felt judged. She felt stressed. She felt burdened with guilt and, most particularly, shame if it was *wrong*. And terrified of not getting that all-important teacher approval. The eventual outcome of which was that she became terrified of even *having a go*.

Before she started school, she loved drawing. A few years of trying to draw it *right* in school, of being told (at seven years of age) that if her drawing didn't look exactly like a particular thing then it was no good, destroyed that love of hers. Even six years later the legacy of that regime meant that drawing could still reduce her to tears. And she never drew for fun or from imagination any more.

In some schools even guesses have to be right. Being right is the rule. That is the only way to get ahead. Doing things wrong is packed with shame and humiliation.

Her sister, who only did the first reception year in school, had a completely different approach.

She hadn't had time to feel ashamed by being wrong. Since we only ever encouraged her to *have a go* whatever the outcome, she wasn't so afraid of 'wrong'. She'd been shown that *whatever the outcome* there is something to be *learned* from it, wrong or not.

Therefore she had the confidence to make guesses, try alternatives, break rules, find ways forward whether they be right or not. Even do them badly if that is the outcome of having a go. Because once you've had a go and made mistakes, you can then see the right way forward.

You make lots of fascinating discoveries. You learn heaps more than on the straight and *correct* path.

This was all proved to me with a computer game the children liked playing. It was a maths one with a kind of adventure that took the player through various mathematical concepts to gain the golden coins. It wasn't something I considered to be particularly valuable, but they liked playing it and meanwhile some of the maths seeped in.

One day, my eldest said. 'It's not fair. How come she can get to the end and get all the golden coins when I can hardly get past the first hurdle? And she's three years younger than me!'

I thought about it. Thought how they both worked it. Then I realised; it wasn't to do with their mathematical development. It was to do with having the courage to take the risk of being wrong.

'It's only because she is prepared to do it wrong!' I said. 'She makes guesses. She has a go at anything. She clicks any old answer until she gets through. She makes lots of mistakes, then puts them right. That's how she does it. But you are worried about putting in a wrong answer and will only ever put one in if you're sure it's right. You don't like to risk it. So if you're not sure of the correct answer you get stuck!'

We talked a lot more about right and wrong. About the *value* of making mistakes, that there's no shame attached. How mistakes can eventually sort out the right answer for you. About just having a go—whatever. And we talked about all the amazing discoveries and the scientists, adventurers and business people who have succeeded by just having a go, not even knowing whether they were right or not, doing it wrong first off, then finding a better solution as a result.

Then we set her a new way to work; to just have a go whatever. Whether maths or art, right or wrong. And I suggested she put aside a time to draw *badly*!

We had a good laugh over that.

But actually, it's serious. It is seriously sad that our learning culture puts so much emphasis on always being right, consequently inhibiting valuable learning.

Being brave enough to be wrong sometimes teaches our children so much—us too. Sometimes learning requires us to take risks. This is often how new discoveries are made. And it also gives them something even more important; the confidence they need to tackle things, even difficult things when it's going to take several attempts to get it right.

Giving our children confidence is the greatest thing we can do for them. And the home educating days that were the most amazing of all were the days when they just had a go, had the confidence and stamina to push through their mistakes and bungles, not feel any shame or give up, and finally achieve something they never thought they could. *Confidence*, despite getting it wrong, is what they need. That's why getting it wrong is sometimes the right thing to do.

The brilliance of home education is that it affords as many goes at getting it wrong as children need.

27

TESTING? FORGET IT AND GET ON WITH THE LEARNING

Parents can get obsessed with testing—we've been taught to. So you might be thinking that you cannot home educate without doing so.

This is why I thought I'd tell you something: our children went through the whole of their home educating lives without doing a test.

Okay, that might not be completely true; there were swimming tests and dancing tests and drama and scuba diving exams, do they count? Otherwise, they never did any academic tests at home.

But here's something else you might welcome knowing: they still dealt with them perfectly well when they went to college and achieved distinctions in their subjects and awards for 'Learner of the Year' etc.

I have to say though, that I think they might have got that award because, not having been to school, I reckon the college made the assumption that they wouldn't be able to do anything and got a bit of a shock!

Then they both went onto pass their driving tests when they were older, and deal with interviews for unis and jobs and other sorts of test situations that people think youngsters are not going to be able to cope with if they don't endure the misery of being constantly tested and examined throughout their educative years.

I'd like to tell you that idea is complete balderdash! Children don't need constant testing in order to cope with tests or exams, they just need a bit of practice. And they don't need to be put under stress in order to cope with stress—they need other approaches, understanding and maturity for them to cope with it.

We never bought into these kinds of ideas: firstly, that life is going to be misery so the kids better get used to it by education being misery, and secondly, that testing and examining throughout school life is useful.

It isn't, not for the learner, not for preparation of a learner for life, and not because the results have any kind of value attached to them at all.

Kids and parents are dragged through the system of testing as if it's an educational panacea, when it is in fact an educational slurry pit. It wastes everyone's time and energy and sullies the real process of education. Here are a few ideas to explain why:

For starters; what do the results show?

Do they really show that a child is good at something or just that the child did well at the subject on that day? And conversely, does a poor result show that a child doesn't know the subject, or just that they're useless at tests? What is it that's being tested? Are we testing true intelligent understanding or just a performance?

And what value is all that anyway?

What *is* of real value is whether the youngsters can *use* their knowledge and skills in a *real* setting, not just for test passing. You also have to acknowledge that there are youngsters who have the potential to be brilliant scientists, but could also be dyslexic, so they're never going to get good results on a test paper. So how best to help them get where they need to go? Tests won't do it.

Another consideration; testing is a dangerous part of the cloning procedure which purports that children should be all the same. Children are *not* the same. Children mature into different understanding all at different rates, so testing every child for the same thing at the same age is ludicrous.

Another question; what use is testing to the learner? On occasions, if a test is imminent, it serves to have some practice at the experience so you know what to expect. That might be of use to a learner. Another use might be to test your own knowledge and skills as part of a self-development procedure where you're interested in the results, where you might want to assess a shortfall, or adjust your learning in the future as a result.

But this is rarely how testing is used by most parents.

Testing is mostly used as a form of one-upmanship or social snobbery. Or reassurance perhaps that maybe you're doing okay.

None of this is healthy.

One-upmanship or social status has *no place* in the personal education of an individual. Am I the only one who sees the public display of test and exam results as an absolutely abhorrent practice which proves the point about one-upmanship? Shame can also be a tragic outcome.

And unfortunately, there are no assurances anywhere, because a test on one day is not necessarily going to be the same on another.

Testing throughout a child's school life is totally unnecessary. It is performed really because people want some kind of tangible results and they think testing gives them that. But once you consider the points I've raised above, I think you'll see that testing is pretty worthless.

When I'm in a really cynical mood I also think that testing is just another strategy politicians use to impress parents, our children merely pawns in their vote-winning game.

I'm not suggesting that all testing is abandoned from all forms of education forever. It's just that so many parents have been conned by the big school machine to think that testing is a valuable and necessary part of a child's education. It isn't. Children can get on equally well in life without it.

What testing is, is just another *tool* in your toolbox, to use if it's useful to you and what you do. But it will only be useful if you're *clear* about what you're using it *for*, you're clear about what the results are going to *tell you*, and clear about how you can use the results to *further your child's education.*

In this way testing can become a part of an educational approach, not an education in itself, nor the proof of one. The only proof, and the only assurance you'll ever have will be when your children are grown up and doing the things they want to do, achieving and happy as I'm sure you want them to be. You really do have to wait that long to know it's going to be all right—tests won't guarantee anything. Sorry!

So, in compensation for that wobbly news, I'm offering you some reassurance by way of knowing that I came across many home educated youngsters who did *none* of the standard school style tests during their learning lives at home, yet who still went on to achieve good grades, and jobs and decent happy lives.

These youngsters, now graduating, are living proof that you don't need testing throughout your school life. It is a waste of a learner's time, it heaps unnecessary stress on everyone concerned, it labels and creates sometimes disastrous self-fulfilling prophecies.

So, I shouldn't waste time with them if I were you. Instead, get on with the far more important job of giving your children deep and meaningful, varied, fun and stimulating educational experiences.

In other words, get on with the real learning, not the testing of it.

28

Thoughtful Mud Pies!

There was one activity my youngest used to love that worried me.

Well, there were a lot of things I suppose, such is the nature of parenting! But this particular activity just seemed a step too weird and I wondered if I should stop her.

Other children didn't seem to do it much. And it was the reason that a little friend was banned from playing with mine anymore.

It happened in a disastrous moment when I was busy in the kitchen knowing the two of them were happily playing out—I could hear them and see them from the window. I looked away a moment and then heard screaming coming from the drive. I ran out, fearing the worst, to discover it was the mother doing the screaming, over a bit of mud her child had splattered on her shoes. And the fact her child's hands were muddy.

They would be, they'd been having a wonderful afternoon making mud pies. How the friend had managed to keep so clean I've no idea. Mine was covered in it.

As you can imagine, she wasn't allowed round to play any more. And you can probably also imagine that after this scenario I wondered if I was right in letting my daughter spend so much time messing about with mud, lost in a little world of her own.

That's what happened when she played with mud. She disappeared into a little world of her imagination and when I was lucky enough to hear I realised there was a constant imaginative monologue going on. It so absorbed her it seemed a shame to put a stop to it. Was it that weird? Was there a need to?

I asked her about her attraction to making mud pies once.

'I just love it,' she told me. 'It gives me time to *think.*'

I did feel a bit better when she told me that. She was only little and if she could make that analysis at that age, perhaps it was doing some good.

I felt a lot better when a friend of mine who is an ecologist once told me how she could see my daughter's attraction to mud. She said that she too just loved soil. She loved the feel of it through her fingers when she was doing the garden.

Mine wasn't the only one then.

And I felt immensely better about it when I happened to read about Carl Jung. He was a famous psychiatrist who worked with Freud. Apparently, even though he had invited guests over to dinner, when they arrived they couldn't find him anywhere. This was because he was still down the garden making mud pies and he chose to do this because it helped him to think.

And there was me worrying there was something wrong with my child. Obviously, I'd got that wrong. If it was good enough for Carl Jung to develop his thinking who was I to interfere?

But the really important point was; it was not the activity of mud pie making that mattered, it was having the opportunity to *think*. And to think up activities for oneself without the ready-made ones our children are so constantly spoon-fed.

It seems to me that many children have little opportunity to think and plan out their own activities, planning being good practice for the planning required in real life later on, because their school lives and virtual lives are so scheduled and dependent on ready-made entertainment.

Children's lives are filled by others. Cluttered with academic stuff and technology. So barraged with various forms of media and mass entertainment. How often do you ever see them taking the opportunity to just think? How often do you see them engaged in an activity they thought up all by themselves—like creating something, for example?

Then we complain that young people can't think for themselves.

There's also a parenting trend to keep children constantly busy, both in school and out. With the amount of work children are expected to complete in order to meet the demands of the National Curriculum there doesn't seem to be time or energy for much else. With virtual and digital connection who would ever bother with just thinking, or thinking up something to do all by themselves? Who would ever bother with taking time to invent something or make something?

To think; what do I really want to do with my life?

Our modern technology loaded lives can be quite stressful. We're always on call. There is rarely an unfilled moment to release that stress. Unfilled moments to come to terms with and assimilate our experiences. To have quiet opportunities to think things through and out of our systems. To think how we feel about something, and discover what we like to do. Form opinions. Make decisions. Discover things about ourselves and by ourselves.

We need some quieter spaces to do that, spaces that are not filled in for us by others, by social media, by virtual stimuli.

It's so important that youngsters are aware of the influences that they're under all the time and it's important that these are *managed*.

Life can become a conveyor belt type of existence, the conveyor belt being the one in charge of dragging you along without a moment's thought. Rather than you being the one in charge, making opportunities to create the thinking power required to control your life. It's true both for us and our children.

And we have to be the role model for our kids.

I'm not suggesting everyone gets out there and makes mud pies but in educating our children we need to demonstrate different ways of leading life. We need to show our children how to practice thinking up activities for themselves and which activities are important to them, or make them feel good. Or alternatively; make them feel *not* so good.

I see some children who clearly feel not so good when they've spent hours on a frenetic computer game that leaves them charged and frustrated. I've also seen children chasing about a park or just messing about by a stream who are relaxed and calm. There is room for all sorts of activities in a child's life and it's worth talking to them about how they feel during various activities and why that might be. We don't have to control them all the time, but talking about these things makes them aware.

The most important awareness is *thinking*.

Any education needs to result in a person having some idea of what they like, what they want to do, how to work and play, how to work things out for themselves. Children need time and opportunity to think about that so they have the skills to think things out for themselves.

I wanted to give my children opportunities to think, form opinions, ask questions, work stuff out, mull over their experiences, come to conclusions, and, most importantly, be aware of what they feel, rather than just doing what everyone else is telling them to do. Because what they feel is right for them.

It may not be making mud pies that children need to develop those skills. (It's not what I do when I want to think either). It may be playing. It might be building or listening to music, or making pictures. It may be just lying on the bed. But they must have opportunities to think for themselves. To think what they feel. Opportunities for headspace.

And we shouldn't be afraid of the time they spend doing that. We needn't be afraid that they are bored and quickly get them busy. Bored time is good. Bored is their problem, not our fault. Bored is something *they* can do something about if they think hard enough about it. Bored gives children time to think out their own solutions. That time is valuable. It helps them find out their own thoughts, instead of thinking other people's thoughts. It helps them find their own way.

So, I did allow her to go on making mud pies as long as she wanted. It went right onto teenhood and into pottery classes. But thanks to Carl Jung I didn't bother about it anymore. It stopped in the end but she did mention to me the other day, when we were remembering, how she missed it because it was so relaxing.

Perhaps we should all give it a try!

29

ALL CHILDREN NEED

'We couldn't possibly home educate; we don't have the money or the resources.' I've heard this from other parents on several occasions.

It illustrates another misconception that many are under—that you need a lot of special resources to educate a child.

As the education system has developed it has led us to believe that. It's almost brainwashed us to think that educating a child is something we couldn't possibly do, or afford, even if we had the brains. And that, in order to become educated, children need expensive resources, strategies, streaming, teachers, curricula, fancy equipment and exams.

These things can be useful. But they are not basically what children need.

As we home educated I realised that children actually need something much more fundamental than that. Something much more simple and realistic. And something which almost *anybody* can provide. And the further I've come away from the idea of education only being accessible in school the more I actually see that process as akin to battery farming.

Battery farms are places where large numbers of chickens can be tended by an extremely small number of carers yet still achieve a high output of eggs. This makes it more profitable.

Call me a cynic if you like, but it seems schools have become alarmingly similar. They are set up to drill large numbers of children down the same narrow route so they produce the same required results.

But this is not what children need (neither do chickens come to that). Children need a more nurturing environment, where they have their individual strengths recognised and developed and their weak areas supported. Take care of the child and the results will take care of themselves, I feel.

For I have never wholly believed that children are *born* underachievers.

I think *schools make* underachievers by failing to acknowledge the fact that children have these individual strengths and weaknesses and thus particular needs, including the opportunity to develop as individuals. And were these needs better supported in a holistic learning environment their education, intelligence and emotional development would flourish.

I've always believed instead, as I've watched children become educated both in school and out of it, that the most fundamental resource our children need is the *time and attention of another human being.*

Education and learning is greatly dependent on the successful *interaction* between human beings. Individual human beings—with differences.

Treating our children like chickens in a battery farm suggests to me that we don't even care enough about them to see that every child is in a small enough group to get that required attention.

The government would tell us that isn't doable financially. But the thing about finance is that if we stopped wasting money on new strategies, resources, new curricula and the latest technological fad and started spending money on giving our children more *people* to help them with their education it would probably still work out as cost effective. There would certainly be less money spent on trying to 'fix' those so-called 'underachievers'.

I feel that if we gave every teacher a class of only about ten children there would be hardly any children in this country who couldn't read, who couldn't write, who didn't have an understanding of basic numeracy or who wasn't computer literate or able to achieve academic outcomes. It's as simple as that.

One caring adult who has the time to give individual attention and encouragement is all that's needed. Not flashy resources, graded courses, or attainment tests. Not fancy equipment or technology; that's only of secondary importance.

One caring adult can facilitate most of what a child needs, with a little thought and research. Home educators are proof of that.

The home educators I know are mostly not teachers. They certainly don't have lots of money or expensive resources—they make do. They are not educationalists, experts or politicians, they mostly don't have strategies, do testing, and many of them don't follow the National Curriculum. They're just people who've learnt the secret: that all kids need to learn is one caring adult who'll spend the time to talk with (not at) them, and help, encourage and inspire them. Children don't even need the adult all of the time as, just like riding a bike, once they've got going, freewheeling is just as productive.

There is hardly a home educated child who ends up unable to read, who is not numerate or literate or computer wise, some now graduating into the wider world of higher education and work. And these children have achieved those outcomes because they've had attentive encouragement from another human being.

That's all; human contact. Or should it be; *humane* contact. Respect and dignity. Not being massed together like chickens and treated like they are all the same and should be made all the same.

Children are born wanting to learn. They are born curious and inquisitive and keen. Then they go to school and for many this desire to learn tends to disappear and be replaced with a general apathy towards education. Often because of the way they are treated.

In no way am I saying that home educating is the answer for all. But those who want to home educate, and those who do, should be reassured that successful home education is not to do with glittering resources, how much money you have, or what you might buy into.

Successful education depends on the attention of an interested adult who will provide stimulation, encouragement, experiences and support.

Giving our children one caring attentive adult who has time for the individual, for nurturing that individual including their differences, for attending to their individual needs and encouraging their development is all that's needed. That's what most of the home educators I've met do.

Schools should learn from home educators and recognise what it is that children truly need. One caring adult doesn't seem much to ask does it? And it begs the question; how much are children really worth?

30

SUBJECT SNOBBERY AND WHY ONE IS NOT BETTER THAN ANOTHER

Sweet singing rang through the house.

I was upstairs and the girls thought I couldn't hear. They'd shut all the doors not knowing that their voices penetrated right through all the floorboards, through all the little gaps, and brought me such joyful serenades to the accompaniment of the keyboard.

Their chat between the singing sounded happy. Their songs were punctuated by laughter. They'd have another go, raising the pitch to a shrill and squeaky sharp note and dissolve into giggling again. More squeaking, more giggling. More 'no-that's-a-C' type of conversation. Then the sweet and perfect pitch was reached once more and the lullaby took over, swinging the household into happiness and joy.

It was a delight to hear. My only concern at the time was; I'd planned some maths, that had been neglected, to do with them that afternoon as I'd come across a gap in their understanding so I thought we'd have a bit of a session.

Yet this singing session seemed too perfect to interfere with, for it was not only in their voices, but their interaction too. Their learning made them sing as they worked on the keyboard and deciphered the music, figuring out which note was which. When I listened to the singing of their hearts I could *hear* their animated faces—I didn't need to see them to know they were animated.

Did I really need to put an end to it, to do the maths I'd planned right now?

I often had this tussle, seeming to find myself in this position quite a lot. Torn with dilemma between subjects and activities—you'll no doubt recognise it. Should I stop one, to do another?

I know there are some incredibly clever people out there among you for whom maths will make your heart sing as much as music. Who can present it in such a way that makes the children eager and attentive and who can incorporate the necessary skills and concepts into interesting activities on a daily basis. But sadly I am not one of them, so I had to plan to pick up the shortfall.

But with my lack of imagination (I'm only human), to get the children to practice maths skills could be a bit of a chore. And not something they'd welcome when they were having such a happy time singing.

So, I could let them carry on, couldn't I? After all, music is an important as maths isn't it? And I have read that people who have the ability to read music and play an instrument are generally among those with a higher IQ.

But why should I have to justify their learning like that? Is maths more important than music then, or is it all valuable and suitable learning?

There are two different things here that are worth considering.

Firstly, is it justified that there is more importance attached to some subjects rather than others?

And secondly, do we always find something more appealing to do than our maths practice and, if I left it, would we ever do it enough in every day life?

It's odd, but when I thought about it, even though we didn't spend a lot of time working formally on maths with the children, they did seem to know a fair amount. They seemed very adept at managing their pocket money, budgeting and working out leftovers. They seemed to be able to work out a percentage of discount on their shopping when it arose. They seemed to be able to add, subtract, divide and multiply when necessary. They seemed to be able to understand and use weights and measures and time and they liked making charts and graphs, collecting data and plotting points. They enjoyed a maths site on the computer involving all the maths skills you'd come across in school and they also worked the BBC learning sites.

So when I thought about it in that way, they actually seemed to be numerate even though we didn't 'do' a lot of formal maths. Funny, that! They really did seem to be learning as much maths through the course of their everyday lives as when we paid particular attention to it.

But it does seem true that, in our educational society, maths is rated more highly than music. Just as English is considered more important than art. Or doing science more important than doing cookery. There does seem to be a learning pecking order that values some learning over others.

Agreed, children need to be numerate. For being so equips them well for their life in the world. It gives them skills that they possibly need every day.

But actually, if I think about my life, I realise I need to cook every day and understand the nutritional value of food and what keeps me healthy.

I also need to be enormously creative, not exactly creating artworks, but just in order to live my life, raise my family and generate an income. As we all do. And I don't think a day goes past when music doesn't affect my life.

I also need to be able to drive the car. Something I have to do every day, living in the rural location that we do. In fact, I could manage my life quite well without being grammatically correct but I couldn't manage it without driving skills. I could manage very well without knowing Pythagoras' Theorem, since I'm not pursuing a career in maths, but I couldn't manage without computer skills or using my mobile efficiently.

So, who's to say what's important or not?

Do you know, I sometimes wonder whether it's less to do with educational value—what's of real value to a person—and more to do with snobbery!

We are all under pressure from judgement. And the snobbery.

The literate look down on the illiterate. The numerate look down on the innumerate. The gifted look down on the less gifted. The scientific look down on everybody as idiots. And probably at the bottom of the pile come the arts. There does seem to be a hierarchy of subjects. And if you've got maths and English among your collection of exam passes you may well be judged more highly than if you didn't.

But the real truth is that *not* having maths and English among your collection of subjects doesn't necessarily make you any *less* intelligent or capable a person than someone who does. And it doesn't make you any less able to enjoy a happy and successful life.

Wouldn't it be lovely if we could alter this judgement? If we could end the snobbery? And show the world that all different people are intelligent in different ways—whatever subjects they've studied—and no one subject is better than the other.

For what is important is not so much *what* you learnt, but that you *can* learn and are still able and keen to do so.

The skills the children were practising while they were having fun with their music will be skills that they can equally apply to their maths when they get around to it. The skills they use when they are creating something can equally be applied to using a language. And cookery is science—actually, nearly everything is science. It all overlaps. It doesn't have to be segregated in order of importance, or put into some kind of learning hierarchy.

All learning activity and skills, all learning content, increases learning development across all subjects. And it increases maturity and intelligence.

So, as for the music and maths in our house, I realised it was *all* important. *Diversity* of learning and of experience was important. And anyway, there is maths even within music, fractions for one thing.

We need to keep an eye on what skills our children need to lead good and happy lives and qualification may come into that. But, often we don't need to consider that till much later and one is not necessarily more important than the other, it depends what you want to do.

And we perhaps could do with remembering that being able to make your own heart sing is as valuable a life skill as any.

31

BULLYING AND EDUCATION

I have a terrible admission to make—I hope you won't judge me too harshly. I bullied my child into cleaning her teeth when she was little. I'm thoroughly ashamed. But at the time I just couldn't think of another way to get her to do it and I knew the longer term consequences were important.

I'd tried reason. I'd explained, tried to make it a fun game and left it for some time in the hope it would correct itself. Her older sister cajoled as she cleaned hers. In the end I got cross on occasion and 'made' her—or bullied her is another way of looking at it.

She says now (at 22), when I asked if she remembered, she felt it was a terrible intrusion into her person having me clean her teeth, but she forgives me, we even laughed about it. But although bullying *is* an intrusion and an abuse, sometimes, like with this example, we feel it's justified.

That is, of course, questionable, depending on our parenting philosophies. However, I think we all can end up 'bullying' our children at some point. We'd certainly grab and drag our kids back from running under a car. It's a gut reaction on our part even if it is bullying. (I'll return to that gut reaction in a bit).

Many of us will have been on the receiving end of bullying far more severe than this, both as children and adults, perhaps in the home, more often in school. Bullying in school is a common reason parents turn to home education.

Dr Paula Rothermel, who conducted some extensive research[1] into home education at the University of Durham, found over half of the parents she interviewed turned to home education because of school related problems, bullying being among them. And bullying in school is a common subject on home education forums where parents discuss their child's experiences in mainstream education.

Sometimes the children manage to talk about it. Sometimes they don't. Often, what's even harder to talk about is the subversive type of bullying that isn't quite so visible and is inflicted on a child through abusive teaching in the form of sarcasm, humiliation, orders, or so-called banter. Young people are circumstantially powerless to deal with it.

It's a very difficult, sensitive and emotive subject for children to cope with on their own anyway, wherever they are. It can make them feel utterly powerless. The effects last far beyond the actual events and inhibit self-esteem, confidence, the ability to function socially, even going out of the house. The consequences can be so harmful that they influence many aspects of their normal lives and the decisions they make.

What's even more insidious is cyber bullying which can still be influential when a bullied child is taken out of a school situation, or is home educated from the outset. Most of our home educated children participate in other out of school activities so it's possible they'll come up against bullying in some form at some point.

The Bullying UK website[2] has plenty of tips and advice for parents about what you can do if you're concerned and, although most of these are school related, there is also a section dealing with cyber bullying and what to do about it. Any minority group, particularly if they're doing something different to the mainstream like home educated children, can be a target. So, it's worth taking a look; the site gives you signs to look out for and how to help.

If you're new to home education, and you've turned to it because your child was bullied at school, you will probably want to focus on your child's healing and well-being for some considerable time, rather than any intense academic activity. Don't worry if you're approached by the LA requesting your educational intentions, you can remind them of what your child's been through, that it will take some time for your child and your family to adjust and building your child's confidence is your priority for the time being. On the excellent website Ed Yourself[3] it says that the law supports families in doing this. The Authority is certainly *not* allowed to *bully you* (the FAQs on this site show what it can and cannot do) and if you familiarise yourself with your rights on this issue you'll be able to stay on your child's side and do what's best for them.

Another effect of having been bullied is to make the young person anxious and uncomfortable in social situations so it may take a while for them to overcome this. Although all the home educating groups I've been involved with were welcoming, inclusive and friendly, they will probably feel very daunting to a youngster who has been bullied. So it may be some time before they are confident in integrating. It could take a while for them to rebuild their trust; it's not something that should be forced.

We met youngsters who had come from school very reserved and unable to mix, but in their own time were able to rebuild their confidence in others and went on to be happy, confident people. So, if your child has been through bullying and you're worried about them ever integrating again, be patient and have faith. In the right company I'm sure they will —it takes time.

Bullying from others is usually how our children experience it. But there is another common link between education and bullying that may not be so apparent. And that is through the way in which children are 'made' to learn.

We all have Dickensian images of teachers wielding canes and forcing children to learn. The canes or enforcement may no longer be in the scenario but there is no doubt that other more subversive forms exist; we tread a very fine line between coercion and encouragement, authority and guidance, and our sometimes obsessive desire for our children to achieve.

Teachers have been known to adopt subtle bullying tactics at times, but I think our parental anxieties about our children's achievement out of school also present a danger of us sometimes inadvertently moving towards a subversive form of bullying if we're not careful—we may even think it's justified, like the teeth cleaning example above. However, we don't want 'making' children learn to become our *gut reaction to educating*.

So, it's worth us taking a critical look at our behaviours and our approaches to our child's learning to make sure we're not guilty of forcing our children to learn through coercion, bribery or threats, which are slightly bullying approaches even if we don't like to acknowledge it, rather than giving them good reasons or explanations for what we ask.

When home educating we have the opportunity to spend the time doing this, something not available in a school setting. Teachers have to meet very demanding targets and with the constraints they're under can sometimes resort to bullying behaviours to get the children to perform.

We have to see we're not doing the same. Never would there be justification for bullying parenting, and much of our home educating depends on our parenting. What we can do instead is take a much more relaxed approach.

We can keep an open dialogue with our kids about their education, what we do and why, increasing their understanding of *why* they should be educated at all.

We can regularly discuss their activities and what benefit there is in them, from the point of increasing skills and understanding and therefore opportunities.

We can listen and observe what the children's interests are and use these as starting points for learning, so the learning comes *from* them rather than being thrust *on* them. This also helps minimise resistance and possible conflict by keeping them engaged.

We can let go of forcing outcomes and trust in the process of our child becoming educated and arriving at the outcomes they will need as they mature.

In our home education groups we can raise awareness, talk about and establish a policy to protect everyone from bullying, both from parents and from other children, decide how it's going to be tackled, and include older children in these debates perhaps.

By our own actions we can imbue an atmosphere of inspiration, communication and calm around our learning activities. And make learning a shared and pleasurable experience rather than something we force children to do.

We can encourage them to take charge of their own activities, which creates an independence with learning and the motivation for them to educate themselves *for* themselves, rather than it being something done to them by others, which is often how many children feel about education in the system.

These actions create a climate of respect around our children and their education. And it alleviates the danger of us resorting to bullying our children into learning, usually through our own tensions and anxieties, for which there is no excuse.

And this approach also has the added advantage of creating good relationship and communication habits, which will help our children communicate with us should they ever be bullied by others.

References

[1] *Home-Education: Rationales, Practices and Outcomes* Paula Rothermel, University of Durham 2002.
http://pjrothermel.com/Research/Researchpaper/BERAworkingpaper.htm
[2] www.bullying.co.uk
[3] www.edyourself.org

32

PANICKING? OVERCOME IT AND KEEP A BALANCED PERSPECTIVE

It is very easy to panic about your children's education.

I did it regularly, as you will have guessed. I'd go into a hot-faced, tummy-churning panic about what the children were doing. Or, more probably, what they were not doing.

I could suddenly feel overwhelmed by the enormity of the hefty academics others were doing and the things they had to show for it; piles of written exercises, filled books and ticked off test results. And what were we doing? Having a fabulous free learning life with very little on paper.

Hmmm! I could soon feel inadequate in comparison.

This then could result in me berating the children, making them do something very 'schoolish' which I didn't believe in. Or drawing up a nice structured timetable. Or buying some new workbooks with clearly defined and chronological courses of work that 'deliver' an education in the normal academic way.

It seemed I had to go through this ridiculous process before I got everything back into perspective and remembered *our personal* perspective on education and *why* we home educated in the first place.

It's very easy to do, so don't worry if you've got a bit unbalanced too. After all, home educators are in a minority and as such are surrounded by a huge majority doing something completely different. This is always a tough position to be in.

Not only that, when what that majority is doing always appears to be running smoothly, their children always appear to be gaining the right results with the right things to show for it, namely approval from masses of others, it's easy to lose sight of your own perspective.

And it was usually this that caused my own panic; looking at what others were doing in comparison to our choices. Looking at the mass approval they had. And forgetting that although this can *appear* to be 'right', the real picture as we know it is something quite different.

Besides, *our home educating approach works just as well.*

But we can forget this when we get overwhelmed by that majority view and this can easily warp your perspective.

Remember that the grass on the other side may *appear* greener, but is not greener in *reality*. Investigate the root system and it might appear startlingly different.

Other people were focussed on hefty academic achievement at the expense of everything else, particularly a foundation of life skills or their children's happiness. I was focussed on my children's well-being and a life beyond academics and schools, a rounded person, an individual and their individual life—not on a system perpetuating its own life.

When I remembered this, I regained some of my perspective.

It also helps to remember that many school children are weighed down with a burden of work which in no way suits their particular needs. I see some bored witless with the tedium of it. I see them so numbed that they are in danger of losing their will to learn anything at all. I see youngsters fighting and rebelling against parents and schools as they try to find some way of filling a soul that is alarmingly unfulfilled, despite being forever busy with stuff others deem necessary for their own good. Remembering this helps with perspective, doesn't it?

Take workbooks as an example. When I looked beyond the so-called security of those attractively graded workbooks I saw that they didn't do the job they were sold as doing. When I bought them even the children wanted them too, attracted as they were by the newness and the funny drawings and the little bubbles and boxes to put ticks in. And I allowed myself to be *conned* by the idea *that once we had secured these we had secured an education.* It would keep the children educationally busy. I could relax in the knowledge that they were doing something worthwhile. And I wouldn't have to worry about getting everything covered that we ought.

Of course, none of this materialised into reality.

The books were boring once the novelty had worn off. They may have contained a little information, but regurgitating that into sentences or ticking boxes wasn't a very stimulating way of learning it. The children gave up after the first page and learnt little. After all, doing the real experiment, or going out into the garden and actually finding the creepy crawlies, getting substances out and actually seeing what they do when mixed together was far more exciting than just doing it in a book. It had far more impact too.

Since thousands of school children do these types of exercises I was lulled into thinking the workbooks would be worthwhile. They may have been for a bit, and they work well for some, but then I remembered that we didn't learn stuff just because thousands of others were. We learnt stuff because it was relevant to our lives and the children were interested—we chose approaches from that perspective.

I remembered that the reason we were home educating anyway was for the very fact that education in schools had become too entrenched in academics for our liking. I remembered that we didn't want the children being delivered an education as much as we wanted them finding out for themselves. We wanted the children out in the real world, not ticking boxes in a second hand world. And I remembered that while they were finding out about stuff in their world they were finding out about themselves too. They needed practical activities as much as academic activities to enable them to do this.

I remembered that we home educated so we could allow our children to develop their souls as much as their heads. Education is about the whole of a person, not just an academic performance.

I feel the system has lost perspective on this one. All attention is on filling children's heads in neglect of their souls and in doing so many end up not knowing much about themselves and what they really want to do.

These are the real reasons we home educated, not so we could emulate the type of education children receive in schools, but *so we could do it differently*.

We home educated because we wanted to free the children up from the stressful demands of a system like the National Curriculum, so that they could develop a curriculum more suited to their personal needs rather than a political agenda. We wanted them freed from a limiting, structured and graded approach so that they could experience an unlimited and explorative one. We wanted to give them opportunity to expand every aspect of their personality, their skills and their potential. We wanted to give them a varied learning experience not only an academic one.

And we wanted to maintain a good relationship with our children by respecting and honouring their own opinions, feelings, interests and strengths. Not getting into constant battles with them, for despite those

I have occasionally described, the battles we had as home educating parents were fewer than the ones we had when they were in school.

And I hope some of these memories here help you maintain your perspective. Help you overcome occasional panics that everyone is prone to.

Those panic attacks are usually the result of comparison with others which isn't relevant. Keep your focus on *what you're doing and why*, rather than on a system you don't believe in anyway. Sometimes you'll need help with that, so keep in touch with those that support you, not those who try to convince you that you're doing it wrong.

You're not doing it wrong; you're just doing it differently from them. But some of them cannot see beyond the confines of mass thinking.

Mass thinking doesn't make the masses right.

Just because you might believe something different from everyone else does not automatically mean that your ideas won't work. Things can still work well with only a few believers.

There are only a few believers in home education—relatively and at the moment—but the numbers are constantly growing. And already those few believers who've been through it are proof that other ways of educating children can be *hugely successful.*

Keeping that thought in mind will help you overcome panic and maintain a balanced perspective.

33

Failures, Unteachables
And Contrary Thinking

As I grew further and further away from mainstream ideas of schooling I seemed to end up thinking contrary to most.

It might be just me of course; I know I'm a bit of a contrary individual. But take the notion of competition as an example.

Everyone seems to think it's a healthy thing to be involved in. But is it? For all children?

From what I see, competition tends to create more failures than it makes successes. I admit that a few people are spurred on to do better than the next man by competition and this takes their performance further —sometimes. But this is not always the case, especially academically. For some the pressure to be constantly top is unhealthy, for others it creates anxiety which reflects on achievement, some beginning to feel that it's not worth achieving at all because they're never going to be good enough.

And what about the majority who are not at the top? What about all the others who are made to feel bad about their achievements?

Some children feel they are useless through constantly comparing themselves to others. And feeling useless is a sure way to discourage you from learning.

Surely we want our children to feel the opposite, to feel encouraged. Children need to feel good about their achievements and inspired to improve. Not despondent about never being as good as the competition. In this way, constant competition which the system promotes does more harm to many than good, it only works for the elite few. Do you want it in your home education?

The only competition that is of value is competition with *oneself*. Setting personal targets and objectives to achieve and improve upon is helpful if they're realistically achievable. This is a valuable way to use self-set-competition within home education for example. Home education, in fact all education I believe, is a very personal and private process that needs involve no one else but the learner.

We obviously sometimes need perspective; we need to know what we're up against in the wider world. But there is no value in setting children up in competition against each other as a means to get them to learn more.

Learning and education are no one else's business really. And as such, competition with other learners does not necessarily have to be part of it unless a learner decides to opt in. Schooling leaves no room for making those kinds of personal choices, yet we've accepted that as normal practice. I don't see it as healthy practice and it doesn't have to be part of home learning if we don't want it to.

But, as I said, perhaps it's just me and my contrary thinking. But at least I'm thinking.

Then there's the issue of test results. People tend to think tests are a valuable educational tool. But I think tests are a destructive practice designed by a system wanting to increase its popularity by parent-pleasing. (Read more in the earlier story on testing.) Some like to waft successful test results round their social circles. I'd question whether test results show us success at all. I know that they can make competent children look like failures in the eyes of a test.

But by far my most contrary thinking is about teaching and learning and what approaches are used to facilitate this.

A friend described to me an appalling situation that existed for her child in school. Her child is dyslexic and had found writing extremely difficult all through her school career. When she came to do GCSE coursework one of her teachers actually said that they were not bothering to go through her coursework with her because she wouldn't be able to write any of it anyway. In other words, because she couldn't write quickly enough...she wasn't worth teaching!

Now, correct me if I'm being an idiot, but surely, *surely* if a child can't write well then she is going to need even *more* help and support, not less? Surely the child needs more attention rather than not being bothered with at all? She's going to need a different approach—not the same approach withdrawn?

And this is where home education has the advantage. Because that's exactly what we can do; if an approach is not working for our child then we can change it.

We can find practical ways to demonstrate. We can take more time with a topic. We can even abandon it and leave it till much later when the child may be better able to understand. We can spend time trying out others' approaches to see if they work for our child. We can network online and see if anyone else has the same difficulty and has any solutions. We can find ways to relate to our individual child, observing how they learn best through other activities and see if we can apply that to a difficulty we're having, consequently building a better understanding of our children.

This can make all the difference. The difference between a child who may be written off in school and one who is becoming successful with their learning through our home approaches.

It seemed obvious to me that if the teacher's approach wasn't working and the child was giving its full attention then the teacher needed to look at their *own* methods and try something different, rather than write the child off, give up and suggest they were 'unteachable'.

I don't believe that normal healthy children are truly unteachable. And none are utter failures.

I think we need to keep that in mind. To do that it helps to think about things from the other way round...be contrary.

For example, say there was no such thing as an unteachable child; what would we do for our more challenging children to educate them? How do kids become unteachable? Or in other words, stop learning?

These are the things we need to think about when we work with learners. We need to look at things from the opposite way round sometimes to find solutions. We could ask; why is our learner not learning? Do we need to stop pushing learning sometimes?

Learning can really only take place when the learner is ready. They need a level of maturity, understanding, development, willingness and interest. The learner has to be receptive, comfortable, have appropriate skills, and be stimulated. The learner has to be comfortable and confident.

The beauty of educating at home is that we can take the time to observe whether these things are in place and allow them time to develop if necessary.

Contrary to the school situation, where every child has to learn and progress at a very structured and standardised rate without consideration of these more personal developmental elements, we can allow their learning to progress at a more individual rate in line with that personal development.

It seems obvious to keep saying that *all children are different*. We know that, but sometimes we forget to operate as if we know it, especially when we get anxious about our children achieving. But sometimes learners simply need more time; it is very much an issue of trust.

Having watched numerous home educated young people learn and mature, all at different rates, it's easy for me to say trust.

But I have seen, as many other home educating parents have, children who couldn't write fluently till their teens go on to do essays quite competently. I've seen kids who couldn't grasp maths early on do maths A level. I've seen children who seemed to never do anything academic at all go on to do GCSEs in their own time. I've seen others who fought anything academic for ages suddenly decide they want to go to uni and achieve the skills and qualifications needed to get them there. I've seen reclusive children who didn't want to mix or engage and would rather be stuck in front of a computer game integrate happily and successfully in college. Some who wouldn't be up before three in the afternoon adapt to a college routine when needed. And others who seemed like they were never going to mature enough to get off their butt and achieve something go on into full time work.

But they didn't do it in a school-style way or time frame. They matured in an individual way then adapted themselves to a more mainstream way of life once the need arose.

However, I'm convinced that had these individuals been in school they would probably have been labelled as failures because they didn't fit that systematic and generalised framework and wouldn't tick the right sheets at the right time.

The problem wasn't that they were unteachable—it was the approach used to teach them.

Some people don't have the skills to learn in the way others do. This is not their fault. We wouldn't expect someone who has impaired sight to be able to read this in the way we can. Yet we expect dyslexics to cope with print as a medium for learning the same as everyone else. It's ludicrous.

As home educators we can find approaches that fit the learner, rather than try and make the learner fit the approach and label them failures if they don't.

Meanwhile, as we encourage our children to become educated, we should never ever be afraid to look at things from a completely opposite viewpoint. We sometimes need to change our angle on things. We sometimes need to be prepared to totally alter the way we facilitate education for those who learn a little differently. We need to take on board all our individual children's different needs in order to provide a full education.

It is only our own uneducated failure to do this that makes failures of our children. Most are not failures, or unteachable, on their own.

34

WEATHERING THE TOPSY TURVY
CLIMATE OF HOME ED

When it was the day of the home educators' picnic at our house I could get anxious.

I wasn't anxious about the number of home educating families coming over. Or whether everyone would get on all right and be okay. Or even whether my children would behave themselves. Well, perhaps a little anxious about that!

By far my biggest concern was the weather.

A summer picnic at our place became a bit of an annual event. We lived in a quiet rural location with lots of outdoor space around us and a little walk away were tidal marshes, pools, silt sands and the sea.

In the summer, the group could come over with their picnics and we'd watch the children having a brilliant time of it getting muddy. After which they got hosed down in the garden.

So, the success of this day was based on the weather being hot and sunny. The last thing I wanted was ten or twenty muddy youngsters in my house. My anxiety about the weather could be so paramount I was on the Internet checking it every five seconds.

Luckily, my worst fears were never realised.

We always had a fab time. The parents sitting on clean dry grass with the picnic talking about home educating, as you tend to. And the children running about looking for the muddiest pools and getting themselves as lathered up as possible. (Don't worry, everyone knew to come in the oldest clothes.)

They'd toss themselves down in water, do belly flops, make mudslides and have mud fights. As we watched we'd see them running and throwing themselves down and see bow waves spurt up into the air around them and gradually we couldn't tell one from the other as all the bright colours they were wearing at the start become one indistinguishable brown. Once, when the older ones came back, all you could see of them was their eyeballs. All else was mud.

I like to think of it as a day of freedom the children remembered all their lives…hopefully not for the telling off they got on the way home.

Although I'm sure this was never the case; the parents were well prepared. And everyone tended to think it was always summer at our house.

In real life, it certainly wasn't. We were just extremely lucky. What it most commonly was like was changeable. Exactly like home educating.

Home educating is not a smooth predictable journey, or a guaranteed climate, or ever the same for weeks on end. And, just like I should have done on picnic day, it's much easier to let go of predictions and just accept what comes.

Home educating can have days full of sunshine; wonderful days, easy days, smooth days, with things falling into place.

But, also like the weather, it is full of rain, storms, wind, showers, even ice and frost and snow and everyone falling out. Often rainbows of mood afterwards. But completely unpredictable—as unpredictable as human nature.

Sometimes I could start a day with a normal idea of what we might do. We'd launch into it and suddenly storms blew up, it'd go disastrously wrong, we'd fall out, become thunderous with one another and showers came in the form of tears, more often than not from me.

Another day we'd start totally becalmed, with total apathy and boredom. Then 'bling'—an idea sparked and the children would suddenly launch with enthusiasm into an activity that inspired them all day. It was just as if the sun had come out.

Another day could be as topsy-turvy as a gale. I'd never know how hard emotions were going to blow or when they were going to blow themselves out. The only thing for it was to let go of plans and ride it out.

Then we might have a day of peace when soft climate made life and learning easy, all plans flowed smoothly, and I was left wondering what all the strife was about.

And occasionally, despite the forecast to the contrary, it would snow. And I mean real snow here; outdoors. So, we'd just abandon everything and go out and play in it—it was too good an opportunity to miss.

After a few picnics I developed a better attitude to the weather. There was nothing to be done about it so I stopped worrying and decided to enjoy the day whatever came.

After a few years I realised this was a good approach to home educating as well. For the days that went best were the days when I was flexible about expectations, predictions or forecasts.

Forecasts work sometimes. But forecasts or plans for the day or week work best when they're flexible. Everything works a lot better when you're flexible. When you're prepared to change to suit the climate, be adaptable.

Being able to adapt means you can take full advantage of wonderful moments for learning when they arise. Moments not to be missed. It also prevents you from slogging on pointlessly with something that just isn't going to work that day.

Not all learning can be predicted. Some is, some things work well. Some things are a disaster and need abandoning. Some of it is just rote, gotta-get-down-to-it stuff. But too much of this and we soon become very dull and overcast. Surprises are the best.

I may have wanted a nice easy sunny day for the group picnic. But the day that sticks in my mind the most, the one everyone tends to talk about, was the one that had a terrific thunderstorm as a grand finale.

If you approach home educating with the same stoic attitude we tend to adopt towards the British weather, accepting that it is going to be changeable, I think you'll be much better prepared to weather its diversity.

Besides, children are changeable little beings. They grow and change all the time. Their needs change. Your needs change. Your circumstances change. And teenage hormones are even more unpredictable than the weather. Not only day to day but hour to hour.

Instead of becoming obsessed with the forecast or plans like I did on picnic day, you'll have a calmer and more successful time if you accept that changeable is just the way of it with home educating.

I like the unpredictable British weather. And I liked the same qualities about home educating too. I'm all for storms and rainbows in between the sunshine, it makes for much more exciting and colourful living. And there's nothing like a good thunderstorm now and then to clear the air.

35

Do They End Up Weird?

It's often unsaid but I think this is a secret fear of many parents. It's a fear which puts many off home educating in the first place; thinking it's downright weird and will make the children end up weird too.

Firstly, that's nonsense; it doesn't. I know loads of home educating families and none of them are any more weird than any other families we meet.

Secondly, what's weird anyway—what do we actually mean by that and what is it we're afraid of?

Some of us like to stand out. Some of us don't. That's the same with children too. It's partly in our make up. Partly the influence of the environment in which we grow. Stand out too much and people like to club together with others and call you weird. But that happens in *all* walks of life not just with home education. Cliques of people gang together to ostracise others; that's the nature of unpleasant people whether you're doing anything different or not.

But I suspect what parents are really concerned about is that removing their children from mainstream school will place them in danger of becoming too different from everyone else that they feel uncomfortable, or so non-mainstream they won't 'fit in', find friends, be likeable or able to have normal interactions with all the others.

I'd like to put your mind at rest and say straight away that none of this has happened to any of the children I've known who were home educated. None of them appear any different to their school, college or uni friends; they all do the same things, go out, go clubbing, have fun, have friends.

Let's look at the idea of 'fitting in'. I say that in speech marks because I'm not quite sure myself what that means. I think it's partly about needing to be the same as everyone else, which seems disproportionately important to some people. It's also partly about being liked and partly about living up to everyone else's expectations of you.

I'm aware of people who've tried so hard to 'fit in', tried so hard to be popular by being what they think others will like, and tried hard to live up to others' expectations, that they end up not knowing who they really are and utterly miserable.

Then there's the opposite. Some people do their utmost *not* to fit in just for the sake of it which becomes an equally hard and unsatisfactory path to follow.

As I see it, 'fitting in' is not the point. The point is about doing what *you want to do* within the perspective of being part of a community which is what we all need and want to be.

Being part of a community is about finding the right community which supports you in what you are, about compromise, give-and-take, respect. About balancing who you want to be within the community that supports us, and that's why we have to compromise a little. For the support of a community is a privilege we earn, rather than one we have a right to.

This doesn't necessarily require us to be either mainstream or weird. It is not as black and white as that. Neither does home education have such a black or white influence on our personalities.

Stepping away from mainstream school *does not mean* that you're stepping away from all aspects of mainstream life. It doesn't mean stepping away from mainstream friends or social activities. All the children I know have friends among both school and home educating children. And there is mainstream life after those school years and everyone is heading towards that common goal however they are educated.

It is a misguided assumption that home educated children are always isolated from other children. This is wrong, for most home educating families encourage their children to take part in a variety of out-of-school activities as any parent would. Activities like sports, clubs, classes, music lessons and groups like Brownies or Scouts. They have interaction with lots of other children in lots of other mainstream ways, just as any children do. So they are still a part of that mainstream life most families involve themselves with.

And, contrary to the huge misconception that taking the children out of mainstream education is going to prevent them from integrating successfully later on into that mainstream life, it almost has the opposite effect.

Children who are home educated tend to have a greater proportion of

140

adults with whom to interact than many school children. It is the care and attention from these adults which builds valuable social skills, personable skills and life skills which are so useful in the mainstream world beyond school years for things like interviews, independence and employability. And this is actually giving many of the young home educators an edge on their peers who've been through school and been held back by its prescriptive environment.

Far from making them weird, home educating seems to give them an advantage when it comes to competing in the mainstream world later on.

So, the suggestion that not being part of a mainstream world, or isolation from it, or weirdness, will be the result if you home educate is complete tosh!

Our own children, and most of the other home educated children that we worked and interacted with, were as involved with other mainstream children and activities as most. The only difference was it didn't happen during a school day. They have all graduated successfully into ordinary worlds either to college, uni or work.

Another home educating parent who talked about this with her young people said that in her experience home educated children are a disparate bunch of individuals who are not afraid to be themselves, while schooled children tend to be more homogenized due to the intense peer pressure to conform, to fit in, to avoid being noticed. But this sets home edders up well for life. They aren't afraid to make their own decisions, to stand up for their beliefs. She said that she saw it in her own teens.

Perhaps the biggest influence on whether your children will end up weird is your perception of it.

Having unusual, unorthodox or radical ideas about how you want to approach your child's education doesn't make you weird or mean that you feel like that about all aspects of life. Home educating families still behave in connected, friendly, social, moral and responsible ways, educating their children to be part of the world.

For what is education if not understanding about the world and how to be part of it? Nothing weird about that at all.

Finally, you might be reassured by the little story I touched on in the intro that I relate with respect to the subject of being weird. My adult daughter told it to me; we're not sure if it was a compliment or not but it illustrates the point perfectly.

A new colleague had just started to work alongside her and they were getting to know each other and where they were from. The inevitable question arose and my daughter was asked, 'Where did you go to school then?'

'I didn't, I was home educated,' she replied.

Silence for a moment while her colleague thought about it. Then she said, 'Oh, you couldn't tell.'

Obviously home education hasn't made her weird at all.

36

MANAGING TIME OFF

You don't really get time off from being a parent. I found that a shock. I remember thinking that parenting was the longest job I'd ever stayed with; I was always switching jobs before looking for new advancements or changes.

No chance of that with parenting! And even less so with home educating. It is important that we somehow manage time out, to recoup, refresh, do other things that will rejuvenate mind and soul to keep us going for the long term.

It wasn't that I didn't love being with my children; of course I did. I love being with my partner too but I think we'd all agree we might fall out of love if we had a hundred percent exposure to each other.

In order to keep our parenting, our home education and our relationships fresh and happy, time to recharge is imperative. Never having time out makes miseries of us all.

I remember one particular evening as an example. The children had been busy right up to the last minute. We'd been out. We'd been fed. They were in their PJs and it was almost time for bed.

I'd slumped on the sofa too weary to even breathe and my eyelids had gone magnetic.

Then the little one said, 'Mummy, can you read me a story?'

And how did I respond to this need for our cuddly time at the end of the day?

With a desperate shriek: 'For goodness sake, can't you just give me a break for two minutes?'

Her little face dropped—she didn't understand why I was suddenly shrieking. And I didn't understand why I suddenly found that reading a story, a bit of the day I usually enjoy, was the last straw and my lovely children suddenly felt like horrible leeches always wanting more.

In the instant I regretted it I also realised how it happened. It was so simple really.

I was just *tired*. I was used up. I needed some space. But that wasn't her fault. I cuddled her up, apologised, explained I was tired and dragged up enough energy for just a little story.

What's not so simple is not letting it get to that pitch before we do something about it.

Home educating successfully is as much about managing some *time out* in whatever form as it is to do with anything educational. It seems impossible; for most home educators, the children are always around.

Yet it is essential to have our *own personal* times for space and relaxation. It is essential that we have our own time *away* from our children if we feel the need for it. And it is essential that we have that time *without* guilt.

This is important because the home education we provide—whatever form it takes—is dependent on the relationship between ourselves and our children being a *good* one and it is extremely difficult to maintain a good relationship with overkill. It is extremely difficult to maintain a good relationship when we don't have time and space to recuperate from the demands of each other. Both for children and adults. And it's really difficult to feel happy, energised, enthusiastic, and well when we never get time off. It would be in any job.

So, how to manage it?

Firstly, I found I had to *remember* to take it! Because it didn't just happen; I had to *make* it happen, and *regularly*. I did this by organising the children to be somewhere else sometimes, a time swap with another home educating friend, or family, perhaps. Or to go out when there was someone else around.

When that wasn't possible I talked to the children about respecting one another's space, about me needing some time for myself as they do, about not disturbing me when I'm having this time. That was difficult for them at first, but as they grew and I persevered they began to understand and respect it.

Secondly, it's also important to remember that just because we opt to home educate doesn't mean that we have to be with the children all the time, or make every moment with them 'educational'.

As home educating parents it is very easy to feel that we need to be filling our child's every moment with stimulating and educational activities. We don't. It's not necessary. It's not valuable. And it's not good for anybody.

It's not necessary because stimulating and educational activities do not stimulate or educate a hundred percent of the time. That's not realistic.

It's not valuable because after these stimulating and educational activities there needs to be some digestion time to assimilate the experiences, to put it in their own personal framework, to think and cogitate and vegetate too.

And it's not good for anybody to provide this stimulation all the time because children need to find ways of providing their *own* stimulation too.

They also need to appreciate that there are other people in the world who are important besides them and those people sometimes do other things, things that they are not part of, and they have to respect that. Just as I respect and keep out of the things that they do that I am not part of. This is about respect—for children and adults alike.

Sometimes, when I wasn't up to any motivating or stimulating, we'd all slump, chill, watch a video, sit in the garden, lie on the bed together at the same time but companionably apart.

Sometimes I'd go off into another room and make myself 'out-of-bounds'.

Sometimes, when the children were content with what they're doing, I'd drift off into a good book or some other engaging diversion like gardening.

Gradually, I found ways of getting headspace whilst they were still around. Here are some of them:

- We kept some toys and activities aside that we brought out fresh which absorbed them more than those they were used to (charity shops are good for 'new' supplies.)

- They were also absorbed by the things around the house that I used or did, such as being at the sink with water and pots and pans, old technology to play with or dismantle, tools in the garden, foodstuffs to 'cook' with. I used these activities to gain headspace sometimes.

- I let them make a 'new' den/camp in an unusual place that they didn't normally frequent (bath, under table, shed, stairs), or out of sight behind a curtain. They'd take a hoard of toys in there and picnics of course.

- I'd use time when we were doing separate things to recharge. Their time on computers or watching the telly was useful for this, even if sometimes I needed to be involved. But we have to take our 'time out' when we can get it.

- I explained about not interrupting my time in this way; I didn't disturb them when they were busy playing, so I needed them to do the same for me when I was busy. Then I'd make sure they got the attention they needed afterwards—that bit's important.

- I kept materials to invent, create or construct with which they loved. They weren't necessarily expensive; boxes, paper, buttons, cartons, wood off cuts, jars (recycling centres are a good resource for this). Then I went with the mess and tuned out for a bit.

- I'd try and reinvent familiar activities into new ones by doing them in a different way, or finding new angles like having a bath in the middle of the day with toys, or making a mass of coloured play dough (recipes online).

- I talked regularly to them about managing this, what my needs were as well as theirs and what they needed me to do too. A habit of discussion develops respect for each other which is paramount to relationships, even if it is minimal when they're really little.

All these ideas changed and developed with the children. I could only achieve a minute or two of independent time at first, but, as they grew, new ways of being together emerged, with respect for all.

Home educating is a wonderful opportunity to be with our children, watch them grow, develop and step out into the world. There was never an occasion when we wished that they were off our hands in school. I'm not saying that there weren't arguments and fall outs. These are inevitable in parenting anyway whether home educating or not.

But we're the adults. Managing these moments, managing respectful space from each other, is a great example to be demonstrating to them of how to make life, relationships, love—and home education—endure long term.

37

The Value Of Play

Did you realise that home educating gives your children one of the greatest opportunities for learning that they can possibly have? I guess you probably did, but perhaps not for the reasons I'm thinking.

For this great learning opportunity can be found in something that is not usually associated with learning at all. Something that some parents can get to feel quite guilty about if they feel their children are doing too much of it. Something we don't talk about much because we think it's not 'work'. It's an opportunity that arises even if you don't have a curriculum. Even if you don't sit them down from nine till four every day and study. Even if you don't take them through graded workbooks, do tests or slave away at enormous amounts of academic stuff.

This golden educational opportunity I'm talking about is the opportunity to *play*.

You only have to Google 'the value of play' and you'll get a selection of articles to prove the point.

I recently read an article in the press that's worrying; apparently play is something else parents need to schedule into their busy children's lives. The children being those who go to school, whose evenings and weekends are taken up with homework, after school clubs, extra lessons and skills practice like music or languages. Children are so busy these days, leading these structured lives, that there is no room left for them to play. And we haven't even mentioned gaming yet.

Sounds a bit sad to me if parents have to *schedule in* 'play'.

I don't know about you but, from the moment the children were born, play always happened naturally in our house. It's not something that we would ever have to schedule in. And if we led lives that required us to do so I would seriously wonder if we were getting it right. The idea is worrying. Next thing we know it will be on the National Curriculum and awarded key stages and the kids will be tested on it. That is after all what's happened to the wonder that is science.

Science has become some mysterious thing that is so far removed from real life, and so confusing, that we've been made to feel that only scientists can do it. And perhaps for the more complicated stuff that is the case. But although we may not be able to do advanced science, we all have a basic understanding of scientific principles. If we didn't we wouldn't be able to lead our lives. It's just that we're not aware of science in this way.

Science is around us all the time, in everything we do. We're all involved in important scientific concepts all the time in the course of living our lives; we just don't see it. For example, you may not fully understand the detail of the law of gravity but you probably know why the apple falls down and not up. You know that things melt, that forces are at work when you have to push the car, that it's no good using cardboard to build a house because you need a stronger material.

The opportunity for learning about this type of daily science is always present in the things we do and we can use it to help our children understand their world. Observe, discuss and point things out to them (do a bit of sneaky research online if you need to, or do it together).

And whenever your children are playing—at whatever age they are— they will also be learning about it.

Take, for example, all the stuff in the National Curriculum for Key Stage One science. If you look through a relevant text book you will see that all the subjects covered are quite often the things children would be *experiencing anyway if they were just left to play*; play with water; play with various substances and materials; play with musical instruments; asking you about their bodies and coming to understand about themselves. Identifying simple natural things in the world around them.

Children learn an enormous amount about science if they can play, *experience,* discover, investigate, *discuss*, invent and explore and *chat about it*. Experience, and conversations about it, promotes understanding and learning.

Activities that engage them, that are active, not delivered to them passively while they sit in a disengaged way, that are interactive and stimulating, that exercise their brain, their imagination, their limbs and skills, all promote learning and develop their education.

And science is not the only subject children can learn about through play. A variety of play experiences develops a variety of understanding.

Play crosses all manner of subjects; art play, writing play, word play, number play, story play, history play, musical play. They don't have to do things formally to be learning from them.

The educational play list can include: imaginative play, role play, innovative and improvised play with toys, building sets, models, dolls, boxes, cartons or other materials. Den-making and improvising with the space under the table, or behind the settee, or under the bed. If there's a monologue or dialogue with it, even better—it's all language use.

This might look informal to you but their little brains will be working things out and problem solving, an essential life skill. Playing with tools, gadgets, furniture, materials. Using the things around the house that you use. Playdough, pastry, water, fabrics, paint, wood, bricks, sand, mud, soil, leaves, shells, bottles, cutlery, pans, foodstuffs, freezing and melting things, mixing, cooking things.

Exposure to all these things will give them a basic understanding of materials and their properties—the groundwork for their academic learning later on. But don't make it academic, just let them play. By doing so you're using that golden potential, not available to their school peers, for extending understanding and skills.

It works the same out in natural spaces where they can den-make, explore, build, discover, find things, construct, dismantle, collect, observe, identify and classify. Many great scientific discoveries have been made in this way.

When children's lives become so scheduled and academic, they miss the opportunity to learn through play. Yet play can lay the groundwork to all learning.

Whenever they are engaged in play their brains are active and they will be learning something from their experiences. You only have to sit and listen undetected to children chatting away to themselves to hear how play stimulates their imagination.

It is their imagination that takes them forward beyond just having information and understanding towards being able to actually *use and apply* it, because it expands their mental capacity and intelligence and that is what being educated truly is.

Home education gives a wonderful opportunity for learning because the children have loads of time to play. Don't ever worry that they're doing too much of it. Play is an essential part of them learning about the world and has an invaluable influence on their education.

In fact, play is the best route to an education a child could possibly have.

38

Exercise For Education's Sake

Is exercise a part of education?

It sure is, although most people don't know why. It also has a bit of a bad reputation. Mention exercise and most people groan as if they were being asked to go down a coal mine not down a gym. Anyway, a gym isn't always needed.

However, there are increasing numbers of studies to show that not only does exercise affect our physical wellbeing, it affects our emotional health and our mental capacity as well.

This is why it's so tragic that children are getting less and less of it. School children certainly are, unless they're particularly into their sports. But sports fields and funding, playgrounds and school trips involving physical activity, are all being radically cut from budgets and timetables. So the opportunity for children to take exercise in the natural course of their lives is diminishing if they go to school.

Another advantage of home education then; the chance to put that right.

Now I know there are as many who hate the thought of exercise or sports as those who love it.

I actually hate the thought of sports too, but I do enjoy my exercise because I have really experienced how *good it makes me feel*, among other benefits. And I'm not talking hard exercise here, just a daily walk does the job.

I was never one for organised sport; maybe I was just never one for being organised by others, who knows! But over the course of the years my daily habits usually included one form of activity or another.

I horse rode for years. I was jogging at one point (I think the stress of teaching drove me to that). I cycled to work at times, also great for stress at the end of the day—I had ten miles to work it out my system before getting home. And failing all of that I always walked, a habit that has remained with me. Plus a little yoga stretching. So taking some kind of physical activity has been present throughout my life and this is how I got to notice that important benefit; when I didn't do it, my general wellbeing dropped.

That was a valuable lesson I learned. And an important one to be passing onto the children as they generally copied what I did.

Most of us know exercise helps muscle and bone fitness, helps keep us flexible and improves energy levels. We also know that heart and circulation fitness is essential to overall health and that exercise boosts these. It boosts our immune system too, helping us guard against illness and diseases.

You might also know that it is linked to our emotional and mental health and wellbeing. It helps maintain positive feelings about ourselves and life in general, it triggers chemical changes in the brain helping to ward off depression, increases confidence and self esteem, helps maintain self control when times are challenging and the ability to rise to a challenge rather than be overcome by it.

So, physical fitness can have an enormous impact on a child's overall confidence, something worth keeping in mind when you all feel like couch potatoes.

However, more recent studies are the most fascinating because they show a correlation between physical activity and intellectual development.

Exercise increases blood flow to the brain. This heightens alertness and mental focus thus improving children's capacity to learn. It also improves memory and stimulates creativity and intelligence. It increases the development of brain cells which obviously affects our children's openness to learning and capacity for knowledge and complex thinking.

It has been shown that improved heart rate also improves cognitive development and the ability of the brain to shift thinking and enlarge the capacity for understanding as well as lateral thinking skills. There is also evidence that exercise counteracts the damaging effect that stress has upon the brain, calming children down, particularly those who find it harder to concentrate, acting almost like a natural antidepressant. As exercise increases physical flexibility, strength and endurance it has exactly the same effect on a child's emotional state making it easier for them to cope with the physiological changes they go through as they grow.

Exercise is an all-win activity. So, knowing all of that, knowing it increases their chance of achievement, why would we not make physical activity an essential part of our child's education?

This is why it is so tragic that schools, where they would never ever consider neglecting a child's literacy and numeracy development, are prepared to neglect this equally essential side of their development and education.

As home educating parents we have the opportunity to provide for this far better than schools do.

And the best way to do this is through *our own* attitude and approach to it. To be involved with it and show just how much it's worth.

Our demonstration of this will speak louder than any words.

This doesn't mean you have to suddenly take up a sport you loathe or go jogging or undertake anything else you hate and are never going to persist with. That's exactly the sort of demonstration the kids don't need.

The best way to provide for this part of their education is to try and make it part of your weekly or daily *lifestyle habits* by making it *fun*.

This is where home educating groups can be really useful; you'll be able to enjoy activity together with others.

For example, most kids love being at a swimming pool. Few will be in the water without having fun, once they've got used to it and are confident in water. While they're having fun they're exercising. You don't necessarily need formal or expensive swimming lessons. A session in the pool with friends will give the children exercise without them even knowing they're doing it.

There are also so many other activities you can get involved with, from football or other team sports, or gym clubs, dance or boxing, to more unusual things like diving, riding, canoeing, mountain biking, rock climbing (you can do this at an indoor centre like indoor skiing), ice skating or a charity run.

Failing all of that there is always the daily opportunity for a run around a park, a climb on the apparatus, or simply a walk. Plus all forms of active *play*—the best form of exercise of all.

You can do things together or do things separately. Just make sure you do them as you'd make sure your child does other subjects.

Exercise is an essential part of a child's education which extends far beyond keeping them fit and well. It develops their capacity for happiness, achievement and success too. It should be on all home educating families' daily schedule and as much a habit that you wouldn't dream of neglecting as the cleaning of teeth.

39

SOME TRUTHS ABOUT HOME EDUCATION – JUST TO REMIND YOU!

If you're anything like I was you'll wonder why you're doing it sometimes!

When we're immersed in the nitty-gritty of daily life home educating our children this can so easily happen; our principles and ideas can become fractured with challenges.

We also sometimes need some ready ammunition when we get accused and criticised for the educational choices we make. I thought I'd list a few ideas here to help you keep focussed on what you might want to do and say.

When you become a little fragmented with obstacles just remember:

- Home educating is a workable, doable, successful alternative to sending children to school which develops well adjusted, happy, socially skilled and productive members of society.

- Learning can occur in a myriad of different ways, *not* just the way they do it in school, as thousands of graduating home educators are now proving. Not using a school style approach does not make it the wrong approach.

- Every home educating family is different and is entitled to make their approach different to everyone else's. Learning about what others do and then adapting it to suit your needs is a useful way to find perspective and an individual approach that works for you.

- Home education gives your child the best opportunity to have their needs and preferences met—which they have a right to— and a brilliant opportunity to fulfil their individual potential.

- Just because children are unhappy or not achieving in a school setting does not mean they are silly, soft, destined to be always unhappy with learning, or slow learners. The fault lies with the setting *not with the learner.*

—   Children don't necessarily need teachers or lessons in order to learn. They learn anyway all the time, from everything they are doing. The simple business of living is just as educational if they have a caring, attentive and talkative adult to bring aspects of the world to their attention.

—   Home educated children *achieve good grades* like other children do. They go to university, college, or into work like other children do. Their academic, social and personal skills are reputed to be in front of those of their school peers. Graduating home educators are proof of that.

—   Just because home educators opt to bypass mainstream school it *does not mean* they are bypassing mainstream life or are unable to function appropriately within it.

—   Home education does not mean isolation. Most home educating families interact with a wide range of people, in a wide range of places, doing a broad range of activities. Some have far more life experience than those children in school. Most have mature social skills.

—   Life experiences and life skills learned in an out-of-school setting are what make education transferable to real living—and therefore successful.

—   Thousands of families turn to home education because schools *fail* to provide for their children's needs, both academic and personal. In some cases this has been a life line for children who've suffered in school the kind of abuse that just would not be tolerated by adults in a workplace. Home educators are parents who take the initiative to do something about their children's suffering rather than just ignoring it.

—   Most home educating families are just *ordinary families* trying to do the best for their kids. Most are not elite or alternative, extremist or ignorant. They just chose an alternative to school. In this way most home educating families are actually as 'ordinary' as those who use school.

—   Home education can change academic failure into success. It can change nil self-esteem into confidence. It can help overcome difficulties that arose with learning in a school setting. And in some desperate cases it probably even saves lives.

—   Children who have been *written off* by the educational system or labelled as having 'learning difficulties' or 'special needs', for example, can go on to achieve a good academic standard through home education.

- Home educating families are in the minority, obviously, but that doesn't make them wrong. They have the *same* ordinary aspirations as any parent for their children: to achieve and be happy. They come from all ranges of the social, educational, financial and cultural backgrounds that make up our society. And as such are the same as many parents.

- Most home educated children end up in the same place as their school contemporaries either in further or higher education, or in work or business.

- Children learn in a multitude of different ways, not just in the conveyor belt style of the educational system. Home educating gives children the opportunity to learn in the way that *suits them best*, increasing their chances of success. This doesn't necessarily mean academic cramming. It means acknowledgement of the myriad of alternative approaches there are to learning, to opportunities, to qualifications, to being educated, and making best use of them.

- It is also quite normal for children to learn at different rates and at different timescales which home education caters for in a way that school does not. Home educating allows the opportunity to respect those differences and cater for them and still achieve the same results longer term.

- Most parents don't think much about education. They just abdicate that responsibility to school. Ironically, home educating parents are sometimes accused of not caring about education since they don't send their kids to school, yet the truth is that they care far more and think far more than many of the school-using parents I've met. As a home educating parent you are one of the most conscientious parents.

- Educating independently of the system gives you an opportunity to think what *education truly is, what it's for* and how you want it to be for your family. Education is not always what we've been led to believe it is via an antiquated system.

- In my experience as a home educator within a wide network of other home educators, and whilst researching for my books, I *never* came across an incidence of abuse, which sadly is the time home educating gets talked about in the media. However, I saw plenty of cases of abuse when I worked in schools.

—   Thousands and thousands of home educating families are now proof of how children can be educated successfully *without* school.

—   Home education works!

40

LOOKING AFTER YOURSELF

Life when you home educate can seem all about the children. It takes a lot of consideration and they are our main focus.

But although home education does take thought, time and energy it's not wise to do it to the exclusion of everything else, especially our personal welfare.

I learned the hard way that our own welfare as home educating parents is as important as the children's. Neglecting it, I ended up screaming at the little one to leave me alone when all she wanted was a story. I'd got over tired with not looking after myself well enough.

If you think about it, the children's welfare and education depends upon us functioning well. Therefore, does it not make sense to give our welfare as much consideration as theirs?

It also makes sense to look after ourselves wisely because it teaches our children how to do it for themselves, the most powerful learning tool being real demonstration. Children copy what we do. By the way we look after ourselves we teach them how to look after themselves and that it's important to do so. It's part of the daily life-education we'll be giving them. It's not a good lesson to demonstrate that children's welfare is important, but parents are insignificant.

Looking after ourselves takes many forms. As I mentioned in the piece *Managing Time Off* we have to remember to do it in the first place, to take time just for us. Time to relax and switch off, do things we want to do that have nothing to do with children and education, take time to recharge.

But we also have to look after ourselves as part of our everyday lifestyle, creating a habit of making health and wellbeing important, which will then become part of their lifestyle too and a natural occurrence in the family's daily existence.

This is probably even more important as home educators because our children are with us for a huge percentage of time; our demonstration of looking after ourselves will have the most powerful effect because it isn't diluted on a daily basis by them being away from us in school and having a large sample of others to compare with.

We know home educated children are not isolated and do mix and interact with a wide range of others, but I think it's safe to say that a bigger proportion of their time is spent with us compared to others—we are their biggest influence.

This, of course, is one of the extra stresses that home educating brings and is often something that's asked about by those looking to home educate; how do we manage being with the children all of the time?

The reality is that it's not 'all' of the time, but it is a good percentage of it and however much we love the kids we all need breaks from one another, them and us.

I was lucky to find enough time when others took over for me to have some time out with adult friends or for my own work. And, anyway, I was also lucky to have children that were not demanding to be around for most of the time.

But an extra stress I found from constant contact was always having to *set a good example* to the children. An example of a healthy lifestyle, a working life, a self-motivated example, a good social example and so on, not to mention someone who doesn't swear!

I felt a certain amount of pressure to *be* the person I wanted my children to be, as I knew how much our own demonstration influenced them. It's not that I lived in a debauched way before they came along but I felt the need to smarten up my act a bit—especially with the swearing!

You have to get away from that and let your hair down with other friends with whom you don't have to be on such good behaviour! It's important to make time to relax and be a person who is also an individual, as we encourage our kids to be.

When I had children I found it was a good time to really examine and clean up my lifestyle. The up side of this was I found a healthy lifestyle gives you more energy, more confidence, more positive feelings, more strength, more immunity to illnesses and diseases, naturally controls your weight, keeps you fit and strong, helps ward off mental health issues and generally makes you better able to cope.

So it was well worth it.

Some of the things that I found worth looking at were the food we ate, the exercise we took, how much we were outside and our recreational habits. You might like to look at the NHS Live Well articles on their site for ideas.[1]

Food affects us all. You are what you eat, as the famous programme declared. You'll probably be learning about food as part of your home education, learning about its sources and natural state, why keeping sugar and junk and ready prepped food to a minimum is beneficial. But that's useful for *adults* as well as children. Getting into the habit of cooking with fresh ingredients, finding out a little about food groups, what a balanced diet consists of, is not only educational to them, but will also be what helps *you* cope too.

It's also worth knowing that food affects behaviour and some parents have found that, with children who seemed exceptionally challenging, food has an impact, even some natural foods we wouldn't normally associate with behavioural problems.

But back to looking after ourselves; food dramatically affects *our own* moods and emotions too, our behaviour, and our wellbeing as well as our energy. You can get food hangovers as well as alcohol hangovers, so as part of looking after ourselves *we* need to eat well, just as we want the children to. It will help us confront the stresses of home educating.

Physical activity is another element of looking after ourselves that's worth examining. Active movement should be a natural part of any child's life (and education; see the story *Exercise for Education's Sake*). But actually, it should be a natural part of *any adult's* life too. It's recommended that we have at least twenty minutes active exercise every day. Do you get that—just for yourself?

It doesn't have to be a trip to the gym, or gruelling, lycra-wearing torture. You don't need expensive equipment or fancy gear. It doesn't necessarily need to cost. You just need to *do it.* And it's a good opportunity for you to have some 'me' time. It helps alleviate stress and anxiety and lowers blood pressure. As with food, physical activity affects our mental wellbeing as well as our fitness, it affects our moods and our confidence and our happiness too. It's been proven to help people cope with the challenges life throws at us.

Getting your physical activity outside is even better. There have been some reports in the media recently which suggest that many people are suffering from not having exposure to natural light, green spaces and sunshine. Not only does this top us up with essential vitamins and affect our immunity, it also improves our resistance to allergic reactions. Many people live lives that are disconnected from the outdoors and we've become over good at avoiding all contact with any kind of natural inconvenience, like mud for example.

This isn't healthy. Natural light is vital for maintaining a positive outlook and keeping calm and happy. Mud, dirt and germs are important for building resistance to infections and allergies. Being outdoors is a great stress buster—very much needed when you home educate! Getting back into contact with grass roots—literally—has all-round health benefits and is another aspect of looking after ourselves. *We* need it as much as the kids.

You can probably incorporate all of the above into your recreational activities on occasion. Some might be with the children, but some should be *just for you*.

Many of us will slump in front of a screen in order to rest and recharge. But although we think that this is going to give us energy, it's been proven that the more active we are the more energy we have to draw upon. A brisk walk in a green space is just as restorative. Or maybe you can take up a physical activity or class with a group of other adults that takes your mind away from home education and children for a bit, and gets you fit at the same time. Having others to do things with is a great motivator to keep it up.

Little habits like this may be hard to start with, but can soon become as natural as getting dressed if you just keep at it. By keeping at it you're looking after yourself well; well enough to help you cope and keep going with the home education, establishing your importance as a living being as well as a parent, and setting a brilliant example for your children.

It's a win-win scenario!

References
[1] www.nhs.uk/Livewell

41

So, Where Are They Now?

I guess this is one of the reasons people are still interested in what I have to say about home education, which still surprises me as I'm not actually involved in it at a child's level any more and there are many other brilliant parents home educating their children right now who are far more up to date than me.

But people want proof. And we've 'done it', as in 'finished home educating'. We now have grown up young people out in the world, as do many others like us, so we potentially have an 'outcome' as proof.

I'm sorry to tell you, though, that this is a bit of a misconception because, with real education for real lives, there never is an *outcome* because the children are *not finished yet*.

There are qualifications of course, but we've never really considered them as proof of an educated person. I've met too many qualified ignoramuses to know that qualified doesn't mean intelligent or educated in the broad sense of the word.

Our two are obviously not children any more, but if there was one thing that has stood them in good stead from their home educating years it was understanding this fact; that *education never ends*. We go on learning all of the time throughout our lives, you and me included. You always have the potential for more. More knowledge and understanding. More development. More progress. More change.

That's what we taught the children to know. And, although beyond the ages of school years, their education is still taking place as they grow into their working lives, constantly developing new aspects of themselves as they do so.

At the time of writing our twenty-somethings are still challenging themselves to move forward in life. Both are working, both continue to develop other avenues than those they first thought of! And both know there are always options and choices they can make about life.

The eldest, after all those performances we taxied her to which I described in *A Funny Kind of Education* [1], gained distinctions at 16-18 college, went on to do musical theatre at uni, then into a job to keep a roof over her head whilst still pursuing her career as an actor. She's currently producing a play in the Brighton Fringe Festival.

The youngest also went onto uni, after also gaining distinctions at college, to study photography, but left after finding the experience utterly disappointing and uninspiring after all those stimulating home ed years, and certainly not worth the extortionate fees. She's looking for new avenues whilst working with animals which she's enjoying.

Both have friends. Both have a social life. Both are happy. Both are still speaking to us! Both are perfectly able to integrate into a mainstream world and contribute to it despite the accusations we had at the beginning that the opposite would be the outcome.

However, this still isn't an outcome because, as I said, they're still not finished yet. Who knows where they might go from here. I'm watching with excitement knowing they have the worldly skills to take themselves there. That's what educating out of the school world and in the real world does for the young people—gives them real world skills.

Other friends with whom they grew up are equally busy. The children in a family we were really close to also went on to do various qualifications, some independently at home, some at college. One went to uni where he won a science award and is now working in ecology. One went to college, gained distinctions and is working in conservation. The other is finishing exams at home and going onto college to take them further.

Most of the children we home educated with took exams and went onto uni and into work. Some went straight into work, uni not being for them. One of those is now working as a manager of a prestigious café chain. Another is working in the fire service. There are so many I can't remember them all or have lost touch. I know that some of the Facebook Home Education groups have lists of all the inspiring things these home educated adults are now doing. It's uplifting reading.

But I *never* once heard anyone say that home education was a complete failure and the kids have got nowhere, are miserable no-hopers and a burden on society (which some ignorant sod once accused us of creating). All the families I know are active and productive members of society as any family would be.

So if you're worrying about how your home education is going to end up you should stop immediately. It can end up wherever you want it to end. And if it hasn't, then basically it's not the end!

For it *is* never ending really, isn't it? We have the chances and choices to make or change our lives at any time, although many don't really use those choices. Like the many parents who know that their child is not thriving in school yet think they have no choice to do anything about that. We know different to that, don't we? We know there's another option if you're just brave enough to take it.

There are far more options in life than we realise. But most people don't want to take the consequences of choosing them, or take risks.

People say it's too risky to home educate. I would say it's too risky to leave your child in school if they're not thriving.

There are *no guarantees* whatever choices you make. The only guarantee is that you can mostly do something about it if things aren't working for you. So the consequences of home education are really no different to the consequences of any education; you *never* can tell how it will turn out. You just can't predict anything. What you *can* do is continually review, revise and make change for the better.

One of the most obvious factors which influence this is that education, like all aspects of life, concerns *living beings*.

It is impossible to predict the consequences of character development, personal, physical, physiological, mental and emotional development. It's impossible to predict intelligence, or preference, or even who your children will rub up against, which also has an enormous impact on how someone develops. We can never predict what avenues children will want to go down. What routes they'll take. Who they'll meet on the way. Even how your family life will chop and change as they are growing, which also has an impact.

All these things affect our lives. They affect our lives as much as any formal education does.

But one of the biggest effects on our children's lives and success within it will be their *attitude to learning*.

If their attitude to learning is positive, then they have the tools to learn and grow and change and develop their lives far better than someone whose attitude is *let's get education over as quickly as possible*. Or who hates learning of any kind. Who won't make change or take a risk.

Those people are truly stuck and this is why schooling sometimes inhibits a person's personal development, because it is so very prescriptive that youngsters never properly see education for what it is; *an ongoing opportunity for personal growth.*

By continuing to learn and experience you can continue to push your path in any direction until it is successful.

But then, you'll have to also consider your definition of success and maybe success doesn't have an outcome either...although I think I'll leave that discussion for another story.

References

[1] Mountney, Ross. *A Funny Kind of Education*. North Charleston, SC: CreateSpace, 2012. Print.

42

Plenty Of Praise
Makes Happier Days!

It's totally wonderful and uplifting to receive compliments about my work. It boosts my courage and confidence to carry on with it.

There are similarities between writing, home educating and parenting in general when it comes to positive feedback.

We all struggle on blindly doing the best we can through this unfamiliar jungle that others may have been through before, which others may have written books about, and which others may have even mapped out. But until you actually get there and do it yourself, you've really no idea of the involvement, commitment, sacrifice and workload. And it's different for everyone anyway so a map doesn't help much.

But worst of all with home educating; there is very little *positive* feedback whilst the children are young and you're going through it.

Plenty of the other kind. Plenty of comments like, 'I think home education is wrong, you shouldn't pander to them'.

Or, 'Can't your kids read yet?' Or, 'School knocks them into shape – just what they need.' Or, 'They won't have any friends.' etc., etc. You'll no doubt have experienced it.

What we rarely get, both as parents and home educators, is positive feedback. Rarely do we hear, 'I think you're doing a brilliant job.' Rarely, 'Your children are so mature and intelligent.'

Or even more rarely, 'You must work so hard and make so many sacrifices to give your children a happy and fulfilling education.'

No, sadly, we rarely receive positive feedback for home educating whilst we're going through it.

And this also made me wonder at the time we were home educating whether, as parents and home educators, we might be guilty of being the same with our children at times. I know I was.

Somehow our society has become one that's very quick to criticise and very slow to praise. Our culture, most particularly the media, seems to thrive on nit picking. Thrive on catching people out, at their very worst, and blazoning it all over the newspapers, thrive on TV shows based on doing others down and criticising bad performances.

Criticism also seems to have become a generally accepted way in which to raise and educate our children. Both in the home and most particularly in schools.

In schools it can be horrendous. We've no doubt all been on the receiving end of humiliating and degrading criticism, usually in front of all our peers. It has replaced the cane for an abusive, but seemingly acceptable, way in which to coerce children into performing better.

Could we be guilty of it too? Guilty of being damagingly critical of the things the children produce, in a misguided attempt to help them to improve.

Having been on the receiving end of over-critical parents and the schooling system, I didn't know any different for a while. I shall never forget my English teacher throwing my book down on my desk in front of everyone, after marking my story, and criticising me for expressing myself badly and saying that, if I continued to do so, I would never be any good at writing anything. I was so shocked. I didn't know what I'd done wrong but the way she was going on it was obviously a heinous crime. You'll all have similar stories I guess.

I never knew what expressing myself badly was anyway—and you'll be able to judge whether she was right or not. But I hated that method of teaching. And actually, in our job of helping young people to develop, this offensive criticism is not required. Not useful. Not effective. In fact it has the opposite effect—discouragement.

And just because we are older, are parents, may know more, have experienced more, it does not mean that we have the *right* to criticise those still learning.

There are far more pleasant and effective ways to help our children develop.

Guiding children towards becoming intelligent, educated, mature and caring adults can be achieved equally well by our non-critical example and *by praise.*

I know there's a parenting movement against praise. And I'm certainly against the overuse of effusive compliments which the kids see right through. But we all need some encouragement and genuine praise is a

167

valuable way of giving it, instead of criticism.

Although we can often see how our children's work could be better, it doesn't mean we have to always say so. For continual criticism makes a learner feel that their work is never good enough.

Instead we can be patient with our learners and the stage they are at and trust that, as they develop, *they* will begin to see the need for adjustments to their work and how to develop it *for themselves,* without criticism. If we can just step back and trust and wait. That's the tricky bit.

Being older and wiser (supposedly!), *we* can see how maybe our children need to improve. But part of the learning process is that *they* discover it too.

Once we criticise we take some of the opportunity to learn away from them and devalue whatever has been achieved, and besides, they will have achieved something, however small. More often than not criticism is discouraging and negative. That's what we need to turn around.

We are all human. We are all under pressure from our own anxieties about getting our children to achieve. We all get to the end of our tether sometimes. Let's face it, having several small children irritating the life out of you constantly, or sulky teenagers who never get out of bed or away from one screen or another, worrying you sick about their future, it's pretty difficult sometimes to turn things around and praise them.

But praise changes everyone's perspective from the negative (disheartening) to the positive (encouraging). It improves everyone's motivation. It ups the atmosphere in the house enormously. And it makes everyone happy, both the recipient and the praise-giver. Finding the positive is a great habit to develop.

If we could educate all children from the point of view of giving *positive* feedback rather than negative criticism, which I believe we can if we think on it for a while and remember to, I think it would go a lot easier.

Praise encourages progress.

Praise the small things they do. Praise the wonderful effort they made to draw the cat even if it looks like King Kong. Praise their attempts to invent a den even if the living room looks like a bomb's hit it. Praise their attempt to clean the mirror in the bathroom even if you have to advise them not to use the toothpaste to do it next time. Tell them they look good even if you wouldn't be seen dead out like that. Tell them you really admire the way they try.

Respect their decisions. Be genuine. Recognise and praise their progress and advancement. For everyone always makes progress even if the result wasn't exactly planned. Progress is where education is happening. The one thing that will halt progress in its tracks will be criticism. Progress is kept going with praise.

Keep in mind 'Plenty of praise makes happier days'! Corny, but true! Try it for yourself.

43

DON'T COMPARE...!

As I said in the corny phrase above; plenty of praise creates happier days.

I also found something that does the exact opposite and spiralled me into wobbles; making comparisons between what I was doing and school education.

If I was having a bit of a wobbly day I could nearly always track it down to being founded in me wallowing in comparison. I'd have a succession of downtrodden thoughts where I was obsessed with what other people, usually school people and pupils, were doing and how what I was doing shaped up poorly in comparison. Nothing gives you the wobbles worse than this.

Then I spotted that these big unhelpful wobbles often occurred at certain times of the year, like when other children the same age as mine were sitting SATs, for example, or parents were quoting SATS results. Or at Eleven Plus time. Or when children we knew were moving onto Big School. And definitely when schools and parents were rolling out their academic grades with superiority as if that was the only measure of an education.

To them it was. But those times made me forget that *to me, it wasn't*. Education meant more than that. But when I was immersed in comparing myself to all these schoolish others I could find our education wanting.

Looking back it's easy to see that this was warped thinking, unhelpful and unproductive, and it missed the obvious; I *chose not* to do what they were doing, I *chose not* to do it their way and I chose to *do it differently* which was the whole reason for us home educating.

But wobbles can make you forget that, can't they?

Instead of comparing, *observing* what others are doing is far more valuable. Observing gives us ideas. It brings perspective and objectivity when we get too subjective. It sometimes gives targets and goals, even if they're ones *not* to aim for!

But it is quite hard to objectively *observe without* comparison. You have to catch yourself doing it, particularly in relation to the school system.

Education does *not* have to be like that system to work. It does *not* have to have systematic results, *nor* is it only measurable by such. And education is certainly not only valuable if you are the top, are better than others, or have higher grades than others. And that's what the system ends up doing—comparing and grading people.

The personal development of an individual is no one else's business and comparison with others' development is not really relevant. The education of your child is about *your child's needs* and serving them as well as it is possible to do so and as such it is an *individual education.*

That's probably why you home educate—to make it individual and suit your individual child.

Systemised education does *not* serve an individual's needs. It serves a system's needs. The two approaches to education are completely different and it can be damaging to compare your methods and results with methods and results designed for a hierarchical institution, in the business of producing robotic results. Robotic results are not an education—again something we forget.

This is a reminder to keep your focus on your objectives for *your* child with *your* education and *not to compare* them with institutional education.

Even comparing yourself to other home educators can on occasion be unhelpful.

Home educating families are a diverse lot. Of course they are; they cater for a diverse range of children.

Observing and discussing what others are doing is very valuable. It gives support. You glean tips to try out yourself. You learn from others. But it's when that observation becomes comparison that the danger starts. Comparisons contain judgements, which again produce winners and losers or better and worse, which then can create the danger of becoming competitive.

We should never educate for competitive reasons. We educate for completely individual reasons, that is, if we were truly focussed on the individual needs of the child. We use individual approaches, even if we try out others' ideas, because we will inevitably bring our own personal flavour and personality to those ideas. We customise ideas and make them individual. Something schools cannot do.

I admit we would probably not be human if we didn't get sucked into comparisons at times. And just occasionally it can be encouraging to note we're doing similar things to others; it makes us feel part of a group. It's sometimes reassuring to feel that if others are doing the same then we can't be doing too badly. Sometimes it helps us change for the better. In that way comparisons can be encouraging.

But endless, anxious, judgemental comparison which leaves you feeling a failure is not. It can make us lose sight of what *our* child's needs are and what's best for them.

You can avoid these destructive effects of comparison by keeping it observational. Observe and think 'That might work for us' or 'We'll do it a bit differently but that's a good idea' or 'I think we'll give that a try' and catch yourself making damaging comparisons before they make you wobble as they made me.

You may be doing something different, but *different doesn't make it wrong*.

And if you get any judgemental remarks from others who do not understand your approach, that involve comparing yours to school kids and their results, guard against a consequential flood of anxieties and worries.

You will be giving your child a wealth of experiences. And there's usually no result at the time for experience, just an intelligent, thoughtful educated child later on. You have to be patient for that, but it will come, just as it did for us.

So, don't even bother reacting or defending your position, just have a stock of cool answers one of which could be 'we will see'.

For undoubtedly, you will.

44

Why Imagination Is More Important Than Knowledge

It was Einstein who said that imagination was more important than knowledge[1]. And it's an idea that I've seen quoted many times.

Every time I came across it I had this inkling feeling that it was true. But I had some difficulty working our exactly why, educated as I was to believe that knowledge was everything. That knowledge sorted out the ignorant from the academic. Knowledge brought you test results, exam passes, qualifications and that they were the key to a successful life, so we were told.

This was the mainstream thinking that I flowed along with. So how can imagination be more important than that? Or was it just that I didn't have enough imagination then to see it?

While we educated our children out of school I began to see something different. I began to see where the importance of knowledge lies. I began to see beyond merely acquiring knowledge and being able to regurgitate it, to the *skills needed to use* it.

Knowledge has always meant power. The people with the know-how and the knowledge and the information were the people in powerful positions. Almost elitist because in the past it was only an elite few who had access to the knowledge since only a few could read. Only a minority could afford access to books and learning and the skills to acquire information.

But that has all changed. And the Internet has changed it most dramatically. Now everyone has access to information. Everyone has access to knowledge. It is no longer so elite. It is no longer available only to those in high places, rich places, or all-powerful places. Even if we don't have a computer at home anyone can walk into a library and access information. Knowledge is now available to all. It is something that anyone who wants it can have, like a bumper crop of all-year-round fruit just waiting to be picked. You may need a few basic skills, but it is there to be harvested by anyone and there's enough for all.

If we all have this knowledge, if we all pass all the tests, get all the exam grades, all go to university, get all the qualifications, what then? Does all this knowledge make us immediately employable? Are there jobs for all of us? Will we all go forward into a successful and fulfilled working life? Does the knowledge guarantee that?

Or is something else required?

Why do we have graduates working in minimum wage jobs that have nothing to do with their degree? Why do we have people dissatisfied with the careers they were pushed towards just because they were academic and could remember all this knowledge and regurgitate it in exams?

Why are employees being told that they are over qualified for the jobs they've applied for? And why do we increasingly hear employers state that they cannot find the right person to fill the post they've been advertising because the candidates all look brilliant on paper but at their interview they clearly didn't have what it takes to do the job?

The answer to these questions is simple.

What it takes to do a job, and to live a life, is something *more* than knowledge. It takes initiative. It takes motivation. It takes common sense. It takes innovation. It takes people skills and personable skills, conversational skills and social skills. And what it takes more than anything else is not only having the knowledge, but also having the *ability to use it*.

That's where *imagination* comes in.

You can have all the knowledge in the world but unless you have the imagination—the thinking skills and application—to transfer the knowledge into working situations then it is no good to you at all.

You can have all the qualifications you think you need for the perfect career, but unless you have the imagination to understand what it is about a career, or a lifestyle for your career is part of your lifestyle, that makes it successful and fulfilling then it will be difficult for you to be content.

It is a bit like having knowledge of money. You may know that there are a hundred pennies in a pound and know how to add up and understand percentages, but unless you have the imagination to use your money wisely that knowledge is no good to you at all.

When our children were at home I looked at education a bit like that. I looked at it as something other than just acquiring knowledge.

The way children are educated in schools places an enormous amount of emphasis on gaining knowledge. Knowledge is packaged, parrot-learnt and reproduced in such a way as to make it neatly compartmentalised and measurable. Trouble with that is that it's become so structured there is hardly any room left for imagination. We may end up with measured, qualified children, but have they developed other skills, other less measurable skills, which will enable them to use that knowledge and qualification?

There are many inspirational teachers who work their hardest to give the children interesting and imaginative activities beyond just measurable chunks of knowledge. But the constraints they are under make this tough to maintain. I regularly read in the press about teachers exhausting themselves trying.

At home though, we had a greater chance to do just this. More time to develop those other skills alongside the knowledge. To create the opportunity to question and challenge, to discuss, to think round things from other angles, to try different ways of doing things, to find other answers. To interact, argue, have opinions, try out alternatives.

Instead of just accepting a spoon-fed, knowledge-heavy, measurable education we gave the children the opportunity to explore and discover information for themselves, in practical situations, about subjects that interested them, thus using skills to gain knowledge in a more experiential way, gaining deeper understanding of its application.

They mixed with a variety of people from different professions, who covered a range of ages, lifestyles and ideas, enabling them to socialise and integrate comfortably with all sorts of people, not just their peer group.

And, most importantly, we encouraged them to use their imagination. They had the constant opportunity to be creative, and this increasingly expanded their use of imagination more than anything.

When I say creative I don't necessarily mean works of art. For there are all sorts of things to create without a painting ever coming into it, but for which they still needed *creative thinking skills*.

They had opportunity to create their own lunch. To create their own den or how they want their room, changing it often. They could create their own games, their own machines, their own inventions, and their own models. They could be creative with what they wore that day, how they planned their activities, their own time. They could even create their own education.

We gave them the chance to *make decisions*—that takes creative thinking too. We got them *questioning and challenging* what they first thought of or what appeared to be true. We got them *thinking things out* for themselves. Creating is not just for artists.

Whoever you are, whatever you do, whatever life you lead, you will be creating during the course of every day.

Children are the absolute best creators of all. The more they create the more they develop their imagination. The more they use their imagination the more they'll be developing their mental agility and intelligence. The more they do that the better equipped they will be to put all their knowledge to good use.

The great inventors of the past, the scientists, the engineers, the people who found cures, discovered natural laws and forces and species, bridged chasms and invented wonderful machines and created the Web, they didn't do it with just knowledge. Knowledge was only part of the story, and a small part at that. They needed imagination too. They thought things out, sometimes even *beyond what they knew* and what appeared to be true. They looked beyond what *is* to what *if?* That's how things get invented.

Being creative, not only with material things but with your thinking too, is what develops intelligence as much as other subjects more commonly associated with intelligence like maths and English. Alongside developing knowledge and skills children need every opportunity to create. It is such an important part of their education, but one that is most easily neglected in favour of more tangible and measurable knowledge.

I'm not the only one thinking this. Sir Ken Robinson, author, speaker and international advisor to education in the arts, is a champion of creativity, particularly in schools where he feels important creative development is hindered by curriculum pressures. In his extremely popular TED talk *Do schools kill creativity?* [2] he puts forward a compelling case to show why creativity is so important.

The problem is that imagination or creativity is less measurable, but that doesn't mean it is less valuable. In fact, the silly thing is, education is really of no value at all without the imagination to use it. Life cannot be lived without the imagination to use your education wisely.

Home educating means you don't really have to worry too much about the measurable and you can spend as much time as your children need to be creative and imaginative, building essential skills for living as you do.

Safe in the knowledge that imaginative activities develop intelligence as much as academic exercises.

Just imagine that!

References

[1] www.quoteinvestigator.com/2013/01/01/einstein-imagination/
[2] www.ted.com/talks/ken_robinson_says_schools_kill_creativity

45

WHY HAPPINESS IS IMPORTANT

Happiness or enjoyment is not something that people usually take into account much when considering education. The ministers and professionals who have created the schooling system certainly didn't seem to do so, didn't seem to ever ask, 'Will this make our children happy?'

Now, you might also be thinking, 'Isn't that going off the subject a bit? What's happiness got to do with learning?'

Well, just about everything, I believe.

Basically, unhappy children don't learn well, they're too busy feeling uncomfortable and wanting it to be over than paying attention—I've seen it happen in classrooms. And they do not *engage* with the learning if the climate they learn in, perhaps noise, hubbub, crowds, anxiety, pressure, doesn't suit them or makes them unhappy.

One parent told me that this is exactly what happened to her son in school. He was never a lover of school but the constant noise, hubbub and demand of others began to hinder his learning and his wellbeing. After home educating for nearly a year he returned to being happy, calm and has come on leaps and bounds academically.

Another parent said that she lost her bright eyed little boy when he went to school. Instead of being interested in everything as he used to be, the only thing he wanted to do was watch junk television. After a few weeks of being home educated, the bright eyed boy returned and his interest was restored. Now, the years he's spent studying history at home (they only narrowly covered it at school), have given him the desire and confidence to study it at uni.

However, the real problem with being unhappy is that not only do the children miss out on the subject that's being taught, they begin to develop unhappiness about the *act of learning itself.*

An unhappy association with the activity of learning can create a stumbling block that can carry on throughout all of a life and to have that happen is truly sad. For it means we miss out on the *joy of learning* which can enhance our lives from beginning to end.

Do you see many school children who appreciate the joy of learning or even consider it a joy?

The thing is, we *all* have to learn, grow, develop, and change *constantly* throughout our lives. Life throws at us constant challenges, most of which require us to learn and change in some way, even if it's tiny. If we can do this learning and changing comfortably and happily, it sets us up well for the rest of our life.

For really that's all education is; learning and growing and changing.

All learning changes us a little, did you realise? As we assimilate new ideas and skills into our lives we have to let go of old ones; this requires us to change. Education is as much about growing and changing as it is about learning. And it starts from the minute we are born (probably even before) to the minute we die. We learn and change throughout the *whole of our lives*.

Education and learning do not only start and end with school years. A child learns enormous amounts before he even goes to school. He even learns one of the most complicated skills of all—the use of language through speech. And how many times have you heard people say that they learnt more when they left school than they did when they were there? We all certainly learn more of the valuable stuff outside of school, the stuff that gets us through our real lives.

Dynamic thought that, isn't it? The fact that education is taking place in our lives long before school years start and after they've finished as well as during that time. And that pre and post school education takes place without teachers or classrooms, tests or curricula or schedules, and even without being between the ages of four and sixteen. That might give you a bit more confidence that your children can learn without being in school.

Being comfortable with the idea of learning and changing throughout your life is one of the most important things that will make your life happy and successful. The two go hand in hand. For I don't call an unhappy life a successful one, however wealthy one becomes. Learning is the mainstay of our lives; you don't get to drive a car, use your newest tablet, budget your income or raise your family without it. So it's important to be happy with it to sustain it.

The beauty of home educating is that we can pay as much attention to making learning a happy experience as we can to the subject matter. We can find approaches that keep our children comfortable with learning. And approaches that help them *enjoy* learning. The smallest changes in the way we approach their learning can make the biggest difference, for example, adding more practical experiences or taking them to different places. If learning approaches are more stimulating the kids will want more and they will both see and feel a point to it.

When this is the case they have the best shot at realising their potential. They have a chance to discover what it is about themselves that they're good at and like and how best to build their skills. They have the chance to find out what activities make life happy both at the time and for the future. And that's really important because our children *are* the future, both personally and globally.

I'm not interested in happiness because it's all twee and rosy and unrealistic. I'm very, very realistic and down-to-earth. And realistically I know that happy people make a much better society than unhappy people. Because generally speaking happy people do not violate or abuse one another, they do not commit crimes or vandalise, destroy or disturb. Happy people feel good enough about themselves to care for one another, care for the community, their environment, the planet. This is why happiness is so important. Happy people make the world a better place in all respects, corny though it sounds. Being happy with learning is part of building that.

When learning starts by paying attention to what children are interested in it also shows respect for them and their preferences. This in turn helps to keep them focussed, builds wisdom, respect *in* them, empathy, understanding; those skills are part of educating the *heart* as well as the head and equally essential. We can then guide them towards skills they may need to develop their chosen subjects. It doesn't mean saying yes all the time, that's not realistic, but it means paying attention to that enjoyment side of the learning process as well as the academic side.

You will probably have given your toddler this type of education when they were little. You will have nurtured and taught and encouraged and developed skills within them, without even realising, that will have suited their needs and their characters, their gifts and their strengths. You will have made them feel important and loved and valued. You will have done this simply by parenting them in an attentive, heartfelt and respectful way.

All that can be transferred to home educating, and continued whilst home educating, by paying as much attention to their hearts as their heads. Learning doesn't have to turn into a dull academic slog with no enjoyment just because kids reach the age of five.

I believe all of us, all of our lives, need, and have a right to, an education that is close to our hearts. That develops our heart's desires as well as our heads. That starts from our individuality and builds on it. That values our preferences as people, who we are and what we can do.

During the time we home educated we were forced to think very hard about this aspect of education. For once our children's education was no longer wrapped up in a curriculum and tests and outcomes and objectives and exams, that someone else designed for some other need rather than those of *our* children, we had to think what we wanted it to be without all that wrapping. We had to think what education really was, underneath all that.

We learned and changed a lot of times throughout our children's education. For, as I've said, education goes on throughout our lives, both ours as well as the children's. We came up with as many questions as answers.

The answers are never cut and dried and never the same for everyone. But by describing some of our home educating days throughout this book I'm hoping that I am helping you begin to find some of your own answers. And find what kind of an education will make your child happy and fulfilled, both now and throughout the whole of their lives.

And I hope by now you will understand that happiness *does* have something to do with it and is worth paying some attention to in the way you approach it.

46

Nurturing Curiosity As An Aid To Learning

Christmas and birthdays were tricky in our house. The children were always there so keeping secrets was a challenge. Especially since they were so incredibly curious and had eyes that didn't miss a thing.

'What's in that bag?'

I'd scurry upstairs furtively with some secret shopping and call out, 'Nothing.'

'What's the postman brought?'

I'd stuff the parcel under my desk quickly and respond, 'Nothing. Only some bills.'

'What's in that box?'

Sometimes there was no getting away with it and I'd just have to say, 'Your present, but you mustn't look.'

I knew this would have the same effect as requesting a thousand word essay on the law of gravity and get the same result; the opposite.

So, I'd search for a hiding place that would be big enough to conceal it and that they wouldn't think of looking. I'd settle on their dad's drawers, they wouldn't dare look in there for fear of coming across his boxers.

That's just the trouble with bright children, isn't it? They're more curious than the proverbial cat. But it's our fault really; we've encouraged it because that's exactly what we want; curious and questioning children.

Have you ever thought what curiosity is? It's basically children wanting to know things. And wanting to know things also interprets as wanting to learn things. Children want to learn about the world around them —your secrets included. But curiosity, when it's not focussed on your secrets, is as valuable an asset to motivation and education as you can get and wants encouraging.

Curious and questioning children cannot help becoming educated. It doesn't even have to be curiosity about the subject in hand. Or about any specific subject come to that. Because having a generally curious attitude to life is the same as having a general eagerness to learn.

Curiosity has the effect of inspiring children to learn for learning's sake, without even realising it. And it makes the children not only interested in learning but also come to understand, again without realising, that *learning itself is interesting*. And this attitude is a precursor to becoming educated.

Children are born naturally curious. They're born reaching, grasping, tasting. Put any infant in any room and they're into cupboards, opening drawers, fiddling with switches and particularly fascinated with the contents of the dustbin. They are desperate to do these things because they are curious and want to find out.

In other words; they want to learn about their world.

They plague their parents with questions, get themselves bruised, grazed and into trouble for their curiosity. In fact they are pure, unashamed, curiosity-led learning machines. Even as they get older. Unless of course they have their curiosity killed.

Unfortunately that happens a lot.

It's easy to do. Most adults are driven to distraction by their child's curiosity and most particularly by their questions. And the children more often than not get told off for it.

'Don't touch.' 'Put that down.' 'Leave that alone.' 'Mind your own business.' We've all used those statements at some point I would guess.

But most particularly, I feel, children tend to get their curiosity killed when they go to school. Time constraints leave no room for curiosity. In school it is not cool to ask questions, or to want to know more, or show you're keen.

This is one of the sad things; teachers don't have any time to make use of one of the best opportunities available for learning—answering and encouraging the questions from children who are keen to know.

Thomas and Pattison say in their book *How Children Learn at Home[1]*, that questioning is a form of exploration. Children go through a phase of continuous questioning as they observe, pick up or think about things that arouse their curiosity. This physical exploration is taken over by verbal exploration and an intellectual search for new information or explanation as they mature. And they observed that, although this is commonly associated with younger children, in home educating families this was extended throughout the whole of their education as a valuable way of learning. Most of the parents they interviewed saw this as self-initiated inquiry which had enormous educational value.

As home educators we have the perfect opportunity to extend knowledge and understanding, encourage conversation and thus language development, thinking skills and mental development.

You can stimulate it by observing things around, by bringing your child's attention to things, by speculating and asking thought provoking questions and answering theirs in return.

They'll have plenty of their own.

I looked at our insatiably curious toddlers hellbent on learning about everything, then I looked at some of the uncurious, switched off adolescents that I saw and I'd think, what happened to your curiosity and interest in the world?

It probably got well and truly switched off. How sad is that?

For, just think, wouldn't it have been a loss if Isaac Newton had his curiosity snubbed before he wondered about the apple falling down? Wouldn't it have been a loss if Darwin had stopped being curious about the origin of species?

I'm not advocating that we run ourselves ragged dropping everything to answer all our children's questions there and then, pandering to their every curious whim. That wouldn't necessarily be a good thing. Children have to fit into society and live with others and understand that adults are not simply question-answering machines. And they have to understand when to be safe instead of curious, and when it's not appropriate to ask questions, especially loudly, as one of my children did one day sitting on a park bench next to a complete stranger.

'Is that man wearing underpants, mummy?' I've never seen anyone cross his legs so quickly. He walked off adjusting his fly.

All I'm saying is that if we could be a little careful with our child's curiosity we will perpetuate their keenness to learn rather than destroy it. Let them be curious about everything you do, from the washing up to why we save money or the *why* of anything really.

Even though there's a time for answering questions and a time not to do so, curiosity is still desirable. Curiosity needs nurturing. If we can be frugal with, 'don't', and 'leave that alone' and 'for goodness sake stop asking me stuff all the time' (yep, that was me one day), we can avoid

184

the danger that they stop being curious about their world.

It helps when we remember that those endless questions and irritating behaviours like eating earwigs (one of my children) and posting things in the CD player (the other one) are really them just learning about their world.

Curiosity means they're *keen to learn* and is one of the most invaluable assets our children can have for their education. A curious attitude has a knock-on effect upon all their learning. It develops an educated mind. And is something to be encouraged as much as is sanely possible!

References
[1] Thomas, Alan, and Harriet Pattison. *How Children Learn at Home*. London: Continuum, 2007. Print.

47

Take Care Of The Now
And Let The Future Take Care Of Itself

I was only a little way into home educating when I had a light bulb moment. You know, one of those moments when you see things from a completely different angle. Home educating can give you quite a few of those.

This one was about the way in which we've been led to approach education always with regard to the future and not for the sake of what's present.

But is that always useful?

It was a day I was thinking my youngest really ought to get down to some kind of study. Other than studying her latest computer game. I was trawling through a few books trying to ignite some kind of interest. This was having as much effect as trying to warm the whole house with one match.

She was totally engrossed in the game. It was one of those with problems and challenges that got her thinking and making decisions and achieving goals. The same skills needed for life really. So why did I want her to stop and come and do something more academic?

Well, it might be of no interest at the time but she'd need all this academic stuff for the future, wouldn't she?

Who knows?

That's when it struck me. What about if we educated not only for the future, but also for the now? For the importance of *this moment right now*. What's the point of all this stuff always for the future?

When you think about it, education, all the coursework, all the testing, all the preparation for exams, is all for a prospective future. Either for a 'good' job, qualifications we might need, a career we might want to follow. It's all based on *'might'*, on *assumptions*. And it takes very little account of the fact that everything always changes—especially children—so who knows what *might* happen?

I keep reading about how so many adults seem to have lost a fundamental happiness in their lives because they are always chasing the future. They rarely live their lives for now, for this moment, sometimes not even appreciating what they already have.

When I look at our attitude to education, I wonder if that's exactly what we're setting our children up for. Maybe, for too much of the time, we are concentrating on preparing for a future that we have no assurance of at all. Maybe we could focus our efforts on what children want to learn right now. Instead of pushing them continually into activities for a future that means nothing to them.

As adults, we often find fulfilment in achievements that are based in the present. We might be looking at a short-term future, but the things we are working at usually have some *relevance at the time.* We understand why it's a good idea to do them.

Small children cannot see any relevance in so much of what we ask them to do. For mine, at that time, completing the challenges on the computer game was far more relevant than doing anything academic.

But that doesn't necessarily mean it would always be like that because as children grow and mature they naturally begin to see the relevance of an education for themselves. And maybe that's the time for them to do it, not slog at when they're too young for it to have meaning.

Take driving as an example. Very small children don't really see the need to learn to drive. They don't have to. They have parents taxiing them around. But by the time they're teenagers they're that desperate to be independent there are only a few of them who don't want to learn to drive. Learning to drive is a kind of learning that they take on board themselves, because they see the relevance of it to their future.

So, what about reading and writing and all the academic stuff? Can't it happen just the same?

Most children don't want to read, do maths and write at the age we ask it of them. It is irrelevant to them at the time. Unless they happen to enjoy it, in which case they do it readily.

But I reckon it's not that long before they want to do what they see you doing and by the time they've been exposed to a society that has reading and writing at its core, they see the relevance of it and want to do it, just like driving. Then they will learn it; learning is easy if you have a need.

So, I wondered, could we educate more for this day than for some distant future that is not guaranteed anyway?

Perhaps we could be encouraging them to do practical activities that are of more interest or relevance thus developing skills they can always use. Activities that use a wide variety of tools and intricate skills, for example, like cooking. Activities that encourage them to think out and solve problems, create and explore and investigate, like building a den in the woods. And later, activities that encourage finding out and research. For all these sorts of skills are bound to be useful in their future.

If these skills come out of something the children are already interested in they will not think of it as education at all, yet will still be learning and growing an educated mind.

This would surely be better than an irrelevant heavily academic curriculum that requires them to memorise masses of information they see no relevance to.

It would take a huge act of faith to educate entirely in this way. For my next thought was along the lines of, will children ever see the need to do any activities other than gaming?

Like with using tablets and other technology—and most of us end up knowing how to use it even though it isn't on the National Curriculum!—kids see adults doing things. And what happens? They want to do them. Right from early on they want to have a go at things like chopping the carrots. Lighting the candle. Putting the stuff in the trolley. Counting all the money in your purse. Operating the media centre. Using the phone and all technology. And we show them; help them learn in other words. But it strikes me as funny how readily we teach them all that yet don't call it 'education' even though these are all essential skills.

Basically, as they grow, children want to do what everyone else is doing. They want to have the same skills. Lead the same lives. Have lots of money, decent car, and nice house. And they'll even begin to realise that to do these things they need an income. And the way to an income is through a good education and work.

I reckon that given the right encouragement all children would eventually educate themselves. Whether we're brave enough to completely abandon all academic practice in favour of that approach is another matter—I know some are and it's worth thinking about.

It's also worth bringing more relevance to what they do right now. To make them feel fulfilled today. Not just grind away today for a fulfilment in such a far distant future it is beyond comprehension and may not

188

happen anyway.

It is important to engage them in activities that they *can* achieve today so they can begin to understand what fulfilment is. They need to appreciate what they can do *right now*, as well as what they can attain if they practice more. So they *value* their education *now*, not only one they have to accomplish for the future.

Practising for the future is good. Some of the time. But doing it all the time can create a feeling of never getting there and never understanding what it is to live and enjoy this moment that's here right now. We shouldn't always be saying they'll understand in the future, for always educating them for later may be just setting them up to be one of those people who never achieve that fulfilment at all.

There will come a time when they are educating for a future. When they are taking exams and qualifications and aiming for a future they want. But let that time come when the children themselves see the relevance of it and understand the need for it. Small children haven't got that far.

I watched families educate in a completely autonomous way where the children decided what and when and it *appeared* to be incredibly haphazard and risky. *'Appeared'* is the important word; in the end, it happened as I've predicted. The children began to know what they wanted in terms of work, life and society and with guidance and encouragement they went for it. And ended up in the same place as many of their school contemporaries.

No one can ever know for sure what the future will hold. Just think of the number of times you hear how someone worked all their lives, unhappy at their job, just to earn enough for retirement, to find that retirement totally unfulfilling.

It's horrible to think we might be educating in the same way.

By making each day a pleasant, stimulating (as much as possible— it isn't always!), enjoyable, fun day, living a normal everyday life, observing and learning and doing things, we can make the whole of education enjoyable. If education is enjoyable it motivates the children and young people to be able to carry on investing in it for as long as they need to and helps them see a need to.

And the children will also understand how important it is to not only plan for the future, but live for the present too.

48

Avoid Packaged And Processed Education

Some days I got so tired I wondered how I was ever going to get the dinner. And it was those days that the packaged and processed food I normally abhor looked really appealing.

One particular day springs to mind where my youngest made mint creams which took a bit of supervision, mostly in the form of keeping her fingers out of it, especially when they'd been other places. And the eldest made fudge and just needed an occasional question answering but then went onto maths which she was struggling with and needed explanations. This was much more demanding than anticipated as I couldn't remember how to do half of it and had to look it up. Then the youngest was on the computer trying to get it to do something it wouldn't and getting more and more frustrated. And I just seemed to seesaw between the two of them like this all morning. By afternoon I decided we needed to get out for a swim before I was torn in two, but that finished me off. So, I admit to resorting to the easy option of opening a packet for dinner.

At least I thought it was the easy option.

Sometimes I think the packaging designers must sit in their studios laughing as they think up the most complicated arrangements of plastic and cardboard just to annoy tired parents at the end of a demanding day. And sometimes I think their whole objective in using the amount of packaging they use is to package the entire planet.

We rarely ate packaged or processed food. I like my meals to begin with ingredients as near to their natural state as possible—that's where taste comes from.

But when I'm beyond scrubbing potatoes or cooking anything inventive we resort to it at times, even though I never relish it. For processed and packaged food tastes like … well, it doesn't taste of much at all.

It is limp, lifeless and tasteless (apart from salt), suspiciously full of unknowns and mostly totally uninspiring.

And it was that day that I thought, this is just like education really. Education has become so processed and tightly packaged it is almost unrecognisable as education.

Just as how hard it is to recognise nutritious ingredients in processed food, education has become so over processed it too is losing some of the value of the original ingredients. It has become as unpalatable as eating forced and cling-filmed strawberries in the middle of winter. There is no taste. There is nothing to arouse the senses and the effect doesn't last.

Isn't that like systemised schooling?

I used to think my mother was a bit of a nutcase insisting on buying dirty carrots. Now I know why she did it. Carrots with the soil still on them keep without rotting for ages. Those washed and plastic-packaged ones from the supermarket just turn gooey and stink like mad.

Packaged and processed education doesn't last forever either. And I reckon it turns the children gooey.

I read of an experiment someone once did on a class of school children. They were told they were going to be tested on a certain subject at the end of the week and given information to learn for it. The children sat the test and the expected number did well. A few days later the same children did the same test without warning and hardly any of them scored well. The learning they had processed for the test didn't last, just like the carrots.

Education, like food, needs to be as near as possible to its natural state in order for it to be lasting and inspiring, arouse the senses and be worth having. Experiences, which are the basis for all learning, need also to be in their natural state—in other words first hand—in order to be meaningfully learnt. Learning packaged into a tightly restrictive curriculum, or second hand learning in workbooks, removed from the original experience, loses its appeal just as much as food. Learning and education need unwrapping.

It is *natural for children to learn*. During their everyday lives at home pre-school children learn loads of things. They acquire skills. They pick up knowledge. They do this naturally. Just as we all do all of the time.

All experiences teach us something. Our interests and pursuits broaden our minds. So do books, the Internet, telly and ordinary everyday interaction with people and things. And also our work, outings, anniversaries, celebrations and social gatherings. Learning is natural. And learning from first hand experiences in this way is meaningful, rich, stimulating and retained. Children learn naturally from this all the time.

The more experiences of their world we can give our children, the more we create the opportunities for natural learning.

They need stimulating experiences and new experiences, they need to experience them with others so they can share and enhance their responses to it, and they need to have opportunities for more reflective experiences.

From these varied experiences, play included, learning will result—naturally. When these experiences are followed up by conversations about them, possibly further research if they're interested, then learning can be extended even more. Integrating their research and further learning into these kinds of experiential activities encourages this natural learning process in a way it will be remembered because it stimulates the children's senses and feelings. Like with the grubby carrots that last longer, learning that has feeling involved with it does too.

With food I have options. Mostly I buy food in its natural state. I am deeply suspicious of processed pies, potato alphabets and pasta shapes in suspect sauce. But sometimes at the end of a hard home educating day I'm as pleased as anyone else to open a pizza. When I can get it open that is.

But I *do have the choice* and you will probably know which is better for me. I suspect you might also be thinking that I would be a better parent for giving my child a natural potato that's been baked than a processed pizza.

Yet it's funny how people don't seem to have the same view of education.

Many people seemed to think that a packaged and processed education is better for children than a natural one.

I got more criticism for allowing my children a natural education than I did putting them through an *un*natural educational process. Yet if I continually gave them processed food instead of natural food I wouldn't be considered a good parent at all.

Odd that!

Years ago, children didn't have that much opportunity to learn a variety of skills that weren't available in their immediate community, or access to information like they do now. Many children didn't live in homes where education was valued more highly than earning a crust of bread, perhaps understandably when times were hard and it wasn't an available option for some.

Well, I don't know whether folks have noticed but that's changed. Most of our kids today live in an environment where *education is available*, where there is access to information, where skills can be learnt. Naturally.

They are surrounded by people using skills and accessing information. And quite naturally they will learn from that.

But we, as a society, have been led to believe, as education has become more packaged and processed over the years, that this processed type of education is the only valuable one.

Our attitude to processed food is changing, thank goodness. We're beginning to value *un*processed meals. We're even beginning to see how processed food can make us ill.

I'd like to see our attitude to processed education changing too. For not only is some of it meaningless, unfulfilling and un-lasting, it too can make our children ill.

As with unprocessed meals that I actually peel and prepare, I tried to give my children an unprocessed experiential education as near to its natural state as possible. If we were learning about plants, we had plants to hand that we dissected. If we were learning about history, we did it in a historical setting like museum or castle. Get the idea?

This way, just like fresh picked, in season, unprocessed strawberries (pick-your-own if you can), the flavour of the educational experience we gave them was meaningful and stimulated all their senses in a way that is still lasting.

49

You Can't Buy Education

You can't really buy education. Some people think you can. They think that the more money you have the better education you will be able to access. Some people think the more money you throw at a child the cleverer they will be. Some people think the more costly the institution the better the education inside it will be.

But none of that is guaranteed.

You can of course buy a private institutional education. You can buy into an area where the schools are considered top. You can buy courses and resources and tutors if that's your thing. But none of these are guarantees of a quality education either.

This is because education is not really a commodity that can be bought like other items outside of a person, like clothing for example. It's not an app or an add-on or a piece of food.

Education is more a *state of being*. And that is very personal—not commercial.

Developing an educated state of being is entirely personal and individual and requires something that's not stuck on the outside of a person. It requires something within to happen instead. It requires a human shift. Therefore, it is about people, developing people, all of whom are different, all of whom will respond to their educational opportunities differently, and all of whom will grow a different result in reaction to learning and opportunity.

For a person to become educated they have to *engage* with it *themselves*. *They* are the ones who have to make the shift. What happens on the periphery may make a little difference but it is the learner who has to make it happen within and that's why it really cannot be bought.

There's a saying that sums up what I'm getting at quite precisely, it goes; '*You can lead a horse to water but you can't make him drink.*'

I reminded myself of this several times during our home educating years. In fact it's still relevant now when I want to try and control what the young people do and they're having none of it—quite rightly. I can have all the ideas I want about what I think is best for them but unless they engage with those ideas they'll have no effect at all.

Same with home education. I could lead the children towards all kinds of fascinating activities (so I thought) but I couldn't force them to engage; that bit had to come from them.

I used to get intensely frustrated. Especially when I had all my wonderful learning activities dismissed as readily as I dismiss their choice in crap telly programmes. I used to spend enormous amounts of time and energy thinking up these engaging activities, then enormous amounts of time and energy in the frustration of them being disregarded, but it was my fault.

As they grew, they began to take over their education for themselves and it would have been a lot better if I'd butted out. But being a parent —okay, a bit of an interfering parent—I still reckoned I had to have a lot of input and suggest things. Some of the time it was welcome, most of the time it was more about me wanting control and doing my bit as an educator and, as such, was not welcome.

This, like trying to buy education, didn't work. Because with both the buying and the control, neither guarantee that learning is going to take place. Whatever we try to buy or do, the learning still has to come from the learner.

There is a marvellous quote that sums up everything I'm trying to say here. It is by the famous educationalist and champion of home schooling, John Holt. He said that 'Learning is the product of the activity of the learners'[1].

It's a great reminder for home educators. It doesn't matter how much you do, it doesn't matter how much you buy or spend, or the energy you put into it, real education can only take place through the *activity* of your learner.

In a way, that's quite a comforting thought; it does at least take some of the burden off your shoulders as a parent. Of course your burden may be to facilitate those activities instead, but even that isn't always going to work. Sometimes the children are just not having any of it. Those days you just have to go with it, knowing that things always change and other days will be better. But in the end, you can lead a child towards being educated, but you cannot force them to partake of it.

Canny provision of stimulating things around them often works as a strategy to engage them. This strategy has been described as 'strewing' by Sandra Dodd, herself a home schooler, or unschooler which is a term she prefers, in some of her articles. On her excellent website[2], she talks more about this and other activities like taking the children out on different routes or to different places to stimulate learning.

But in the end it is up to them.

Equally, no matter how much money you throw at an education it really cannot be bought. It has to be engaged with and that's what makes the difference whether it costs little or a lot.

An educated person can come from a poor background or a rich background. Becoming educated starts with an *attitude* not an income. Being educated is a state of mind not a state of finance.

Poverty has been cited as being one of the causes of poor education. But the kind of poverty that really impacts is a poverty of thinking, more than a poverty of purse.

Obviously good nutrition and warm comfortable homes, opportunities to get out and about and see the world all contribute and money does play a part in those things. But you can still have an engaging education despite the challenge of not having those things—they are all influential in degrees anyway, and not guaranteed to have an impact. Money is not the only influential factor.

The poorest family can have the richest love and support of their children and the wealthiest attitude to learning and personal advancement. It's that attitude that money has nothing to do with.

Money can't make an education. A state of mind does. And an educative state of mind can evolve despite the state of the cash flow!

References

[1] *Growing Without Schooling* magazine, no. 40 (1984).
Quote taken from www.en.wikiquote.org/wiki/John_Holt. Accessed 6/4/2016

[2] www.sandradodd.com/strew/sandra

50

THINKING ABOUT EXAMS

Just like with all other aspects of home education you can make choices about exams too. But you need to be clear about what you're making choices for.

Despite what the system leads us to believe, it is not essential that the children follow the same path exam wise, or the same approach, do them in the same time frame as school children, or do them at all come to that. These are the *choices* you can make when you home educate.

Most people don't know this, they think you have to have exams or you won't be educated. Many think an education is only qualified by qualifications.

It isn't; education is something much broader than that, something that I've talked about in length in my other stories here.

But it is the aspect of education that everyone always focuses on and when our eldest reached the age everyone else was taking options and starting GCSE study it was the only thing relatives asked about, having avoided asking anything before.

'What about your GCSEs then?'

This really irritated me because when we started home educating I'd hear them asking other children, 'How are you getting on at school?' Yet when it came to asking my children how they were doing I'd sense the same kind of hesitancy as if they were enquiring about bowel movements or something. It was too uncomfortable, like we were doing wrong.

But as soon as her contemporaries were stuck on the GCSE treadmill she was asked it intensely as people desperately tried to conventionalise what we were doing. As if they must have something concrete to talk about that would qualify our weird decisions about schooling.

And something to show that she was educated. Because GCSEs, exam results and so on do show that—don't they?

I'd long had suspicions about the exam system. It started with suspicions about testing. In fact, it was the reason I gave up primary teaching—I was just not happy to be part of an educational structure that revolved around endless testing. It seemed to me to be the total opposite of what I believed education should be: a broadening of the mind and experiences.

How can restricting learning to the content of a general curriculum for all *broaden* an *individual*? Seems like a contradiction to me.

The only thing SATs tell me about a child is that they have the ability to pass SATs. And is passing SATs a good life skill in the wide world? Do they demonstrate that a child has the skills to conquer the problems they face as they grow and take their place happily in an adult world? I don't think so somehow. I just think they waste a child's time having to practise and regurgitate irrelevant stuff when they could be doing something much more exciting and valuable in terms of living a life.

Anyway, many people feel that it doesn't matter that much when they're little, it's later on at GCSE stage when it all gets important, completely unaware they are looking at it the wrong way round.

It is the *early* stages that are *so* important. This is the time, at the beginning of a child's life when attitudes to learning are formed; it is the time that sets them up for all that follows. So a happy, positive, comfortable experience of learning in those first years is vital.

We tried to give the children a happy, positive, comfortable experience of learning over the years, and then it came to GCSEs. What were we going to do?

We discussed them a lot. We talked mostly about what they were for. Who they were for.

And once we got talking about that, the questions started to get really big; what do we want to do with our lives ahead of GCSEs? And will they help us achieve that? And the biggest question of all; what is 'being educated' anyway—since obviously the children were going to have to demonstrate that they were. And how do you prove it?

It really does make you think.

It makes you think really hard about what education actually is, if it isn't simply about these exams and tests. As once we started thinking about it we realised it wasn't; being educated is much more than exam passes.

It makes you think really hard about your children's lives, their priorities, their futures, what makes a person educated and what sets them up best to find their own way in the world.

Big scary questions!

I hope you're not thinking I've got the answers.

Sorry, I haven't. For the simple reason that the answers, like education should be, are different for everyone. And I believe the only way we're going to get at the answers is very simple; ask the questions.

I know this sounds ridiculously obvious and you may well think I'm off my head (could be true, I admit). But sometimes, not only do we just accept the norm without questioning, when we do start a quest for understanding we can also *overlook* something obvious because we've been *conditioned* to believe that norm to be true.

It has happened to me and still happens. We are so enormously influenced by what everyone else is doing, so much so that we forget we have *choices*. And we forget to *make* choices. And therefore we forget to ask questions.

The biggest major question; is this right for us and do we *choose* to do it?

So you can also ask whether or what GCSEs are right for your child. Are they relevant to your child's future? Is not doing them right now, or any time, going to make a difference in the long run of leading a life? And when and if they do make a difference, is that the time to do them? And how many?

This goes for all qualifications, A levels, Degrees, whatever. You can choose. You can achieve them at any time throughout life. If they're relevant. These are your choices.

However many answers we come up with, there is one thing we will never have a concrete answer to; we can never be absolutely certain what is going to happen in the future anyway. Everything at any time can always alter. Although schools can't work to that premise.

In schools, youngsters are made to work hard at as many qualifications as they can, just because that's the norm, then sometimes find they're completely irrelevant to what they want to do with their life. Few teenagers have a true idea of what they want to do with their life at fourteen.

With home education you can be flexible, you don't have to make decisions too early, and you can change as your youngster matures; you never need to only ever follow one path.

The families we've known through our home educating years have taken a variety of approaches to the question of exams. Their decisions were usually democratic ones made in discussion with the learner about what they might achieve and *why*. Why qualifications are needed, what an educated person might be. That perhaps an educated person is not a person who simply has qualifications. An educated person is something much more than that, even if qualification is a part.

An educated person has a certain state of mind, not just a state of qualifications. GCSEs don't guarantee an educated mind.

Many employers are realising that just because young people have masses of academic qualifications it doesn't make them employable; other more personable skills do. Many universities are taking home educated youngsters with just five GCSEs, despite the competition from school kids with ten, because they know home educated children are motivated and independent learners.

I always had the feeling, both about students and the teachers who taught them, that having qualifications didn't necessarily make them educated. Now that I see increasing numbers of home educated children who are well educated, not necessarily qualified, I know it to be true.

However, you and I both know that people make judgements based on qualifications a lot of the time and to have a handful of GCSEs helps you jump through some hoops, especially if you want to pursue higher education. Many families took the standard five required based on this. Some did them at home, sitting the exam in centres who take independent candidates. Others used colleges of Further Education.

Some didn't do GCSEs at all but took other equivalent qualifications. (BTECs for example, which ours did because they had a clear idea of their subjects—they got distinctions which are accredited as equivalent to GCSEs and A Levels at A* which got them into uni). Some didn't do any kind of qualifications yet still went into employment.

The climate, opportunities and requirements surrounding exams and colleges and uni entrance change all the time. Having conventional qualifications makes it easier to go down a conventional route. But home education is not really conventional anyway, it is independent, so when it comes to taking exams you can make your own independent decisions.

And to make your decisions you need to be clear upfront about what you are doing it for!

51

Honouring Our Children

It is when we become parents that we perhaps truly realise an important purpose.

I would never have said that before I was a parent. But the further into parenting I got the further I understood the human purpose to procreate, to perpetuate the species and to educate.

It truly is an honour to have a child. And I am truly lucky to have had this honour bestowed upon me, to have experienced the magical event of bringing a tiny being into the world and to have had the chance to raise it. And thereafter celebrating every birthday, commemorating that honour.

As we all know, having a child is no small thing. It is no small thing to bear this weight and to honour them as the next procreators they also will become.

When I say honour I do not mean that we indulge every whim or fancy, or ply them with material gifts, buy their love and affection, answer every indulgent demand or craving. That is not honouring them.

When I say honour, I mean honour the very spirit of having them. Honour the responsibility of looking after this new custodian of our planet and our race. For that's what our children are, valuable custodians, as we all are, although many fail to see that or act as if they were.

This new being is an important part of a whole—a whole planet, a whole race—as well as being an individual. And we honour this new being by helping him to learn to integrate into the world, to learn about that world and the humanity he is part of, the environment he is responsible for. How he can join others to perpetuate this honour for himself. How to recognise what gifts and strengths he can contribute to that responsibility, contributions he can make to the world and others.

This is what honouring the child is. Seeing him not only as *your* child, but also as a valuable part of a race and a planet. A human race, a *humane* race. And a human who can make a difference.

Everyone makes a difference.

That is why we need to honour all that is *human* about our child to help him learn how his human-ness can in turn be passed onto others. Learn that he is not the egocentric little animal in a tiny egocentric little world of 'me' that he thought he was, but part of a much bigger human race that he can contribute to.

And education fits into this. And is often where it seems to go so dreadfully wrong.

Education must honour that *human being* too and be a means to facilitate the development of both that *individual* human being, what he can offer, and his position in *relation to other* human beings.

Education surely must therefore be about *being human.*

Looking at our education system it seems to be as detached as possible from being about humans. And at times removed even from being humane.

Our education system seems to me to be concerned with honouring the system, and obsessing about a set of outcomes that have little relevance to being human or enhancing humane qualities at all. This is clear in the way the system focuses more on 'taking over' a child and making them fit into it, than on developing an individual in ways that will help them discover their unique potential, individual attributes, gifts, skills, and personal strengths that could make a humane contribution. Attributes which are not of the academic kind are generally disregarded

In disregarding these individualities I believe it also disregards the spirit, leaving these lovely young people unfulfilled and believing that their personal strengths are irrelevant and don't actually matter. To me, this is the same as saying that the people themselves don't matter. I sense this feeling in some of the children I see in schools.

But in some of the home educated children I know, I see the opposite.

These are children who've been listened to, conversed with, had their preferences, interests, strengths and individualities incorporated into the process of them becoming educated. They have been *respected for what they bring* to the process. This in turn makes them respect others, respect those who support them and facilitate opportunities. Others they are united with rather than distanced from.

Respect has been part of the way they've been honoured and educated. And I believe this is what encourages them to develop a *positive attitude* to themselves, to education, to what they could achieve, and to others. Some young people I see come away from schooling with a negative attitude because they have not been honoured in this way.

I believe children in school need something more akin to what the home educated kids get.

There is much to be learned from observing other home educating families, the way they facilitate their children's learning and the way they respect what the individuals bring to it. How they integrate that learning into everyday life experiences and how they learn from those everyday life experiences. You only have to browse round the many home educators' blogs to see this illustrated first hand.

These records can teach us much. It's clear that educating around daily life teaches the children much about human interaction, what the real world's like as opposed to a school world and what they need to live in it, as well as building the skills to study academic subjects.

I believe this is just the type of education our children need and thankfully many home educators are providing proof. Proof that something less prescriptive and more humane, which *honours* rather than *squashes* an individual, works just as well as school—if not better for some.

In our modern world, as we've progressed so far into replacing mankind with machines and technology, it is almost as if we've forgotten what mankind is.

In chasing prescriptive curricular outcomes there's a danger of forgetting that we need to encourage the *intelligence to be human,* not simply the intelligence required to perform academic tricks. We need to develop human skills, not only academic and technological skills—they came after being human.

We need to know how to live fully alongside other human beings, not only alongside a computer or a system.

The education system is in danger of creating mere androids. Filled up with qualifications; empty of human souls. And in doing so dishonours our young people.

With home education you have the chance to redress the balance.

52

WHAT IS A SUCCESSFUL EDUCATION?

That's one heck of a question! When you think about it deeply that is, and don't just accept the conventional answers that education is to get intelligent enough to get qualifications and thus a good job defined by high pay and so on and so on...

We're sucked into that conventional definition of education and its outcome. To jump to the conditioned conclusions that everyone else upholds.

My eldest was at her drama group with a bunch of other young people who'd jumped to those conventional conclusions, when she was asked which school she went to.

'I don't go to school,' she said. 'I'm home educated.'

'Oh,' says the other girl, thinking a minute. Then she adds, 'Aren't you intelligent enough to go to school then?'

My daughter thinks back to our endless discussions on education before she answers.

'Depends on your definition of intelligence,' she said!

The other girl is impressed.

'Cor!' she answers. 'You are intelligent!'

She didn't bring the subject up again.

We all do it. We all make assumptions based on a simple understanding that rarely ventures beyond the accepted norm that we haven't *defined for ourselves*. Our assumptions are usually based on the accepted belief that if our children go to school and get lots of qualifications then this is going to make them intelligent and educated.

Before we home educated, we handed our children over to school with that assumption. We just assumed school knew what education was and that what they provided would turn our children into the educated, intelligent and happy beings we wanted them to become.

But that didn't seem to happen. What happened was that our children were beginning to be schooled, but not exactly educated. And there is a difference. Home education forced us to see the difference. And it forced us to completely review our earlier assumptions of what education is.

We had to; for, without a school education and school outcomes, it becomes something completely independent and as such needs redefining. Perhaps we'd not given it enough thought before!

What exactly is education then? Have you ever really looked beyond your first assumptions?

And what is it for? What are all those hours spent chasing qualifications for? And do they achieve what they set out to achieve? What is it we want to do with all this education and qualification, where is it going to get us?

Those are the kind of questions we've been forced to ask.

We've also asked these questions because we've seen masses of so-called educated young people, with masses of qualifications, who are heading towards degrees and resulting careers and yet there seems to be something missing.

Some of them seem unsure of how or why they got there, or where they're going. Some of them lack a general common sense you would equate with being educated. Some of them are not that good at their jobs because they lack other simple skills: people skills, management skills, problem solving skills, decision making skills, communication skills, self-motivation, initiative, independence and personable skills. Not only that they don't seem to even be very happy.

We've also noticed that some of these highly qualified people have low self-esteem despite their achievements. And they also lack the necessary nous to lead a happy and successful life, despite a good income. Worst of all, some people have no spark or passion in their eyes or knowledge of what makes them happy.

We've asked ourselves; is that what it's like to be educated?

It's a frightening thought. And it's not what we wanted for our children, not as children or as adults.

So, what did we want?

First and foremost, we wanted our children to be confident and comfortable with who they are and what they can do. If they start with that they can go on to do anything.

Secondly, we wanted them to have the knowledge and the skills and the understanding they need to do the things they want to do and how to get them if they don't, see how they relate to the wider world and how to make a contribution to it. Also, to know themselves well enough to know what it is they want to do.

And thirdly, and equally importantly, we wanted them to be *happy*. We wanted them to have happy and fulfilled lives and work and relationships.

So, we wondered; what kind of education equips them for that?

For that surely is what education is truly for; *to equip people to have happy, successful and productive lives.* Happy and successful is the primary objective. Qualifications a secondary one.

Education is all to do with learning, obviously. No one would dispute that. But the important point about that learning, the thing that makes the difference in our view between someone being educated or not, is not *what* is learnt, it is not the outcome of that learning as in qualifications. It is to do with *the manner in which it is learnt*, and *how it can then be applied to living a life*.

Education is all to do with process and application. And not to do with end products.

Education in schools tends to be all to do with the end product, the exam passes, and less to do with the learning processes which promote *personal* development and equip a learner to *apply* their education to *real life* outside school.

This is why qualified young people seem to me to only have half an education.

The word education comes from the Latin word *'educare'*. When this is literally translated it means to bring out or lead forth.

Schooling leans away from bringing out what is already there, and towards stuffing a learner full of tricks to satisfy an extrinsic agenda; namely to pass exams and 'appear' educated (thus helping to make politicians look as if they've designed the system right). But this does not necessarily make an educated *person*. It educates a person to pass exams.

When I think about education I think about a far rounder education than that. And instead of only looking at the education—as an entity in itself—I look at what an *educated person* is.

An educated person is not simply a person who has qualifications. He is not only a person who knows things. He is a person who also knows that he *doesn't know* things and therefore has the potential to go on learning.

An educated person also knows that, despite all he knows and his qualifications, unless he has the necessary skills to *apply* it in the wider world, what he knows has limited use.

An educated person, as well has having knowledge, must also have the practical skills to transfer it to a variety of circumstances; to be able to use initiative, make decisions, solve problems, observe and analyse situations with a view to more effective management.

They must also see how to fit in with other people in the wide and diverse world. To be able to relate to others, tolerate others and have compassion, communicate and establish good relationships, be assertive when required and be able to make appropriate judgements about that.

So, defined like that, education is much broader than just having qualifications, or academic intelligence.

And it is the manner of becoming educated, and the relationships experienced within that time, that determines where that broadness comes from.

By home educating I realised that it is the processing of children in schools that sometimes hinders this broader education. Simply because schools' educational agendas have become so narrow they place huge restrictions on the people and experiences there and this prevents that broader more personal education taking place.

For us, home educating developed this broader education because it was diverse and included a *variety* of experiences. It gave the children the opportunity to practise social skills out in a real world, beyond the unnatural social politics of a school. It gave us the opportunity to better demonstrate a sense of purpose and care for them and their education which then reflected on the care they showed to others and their own learning and development. Home educating afforded time to build strong communication skills through encouraging dialogue, along with skills for decision making and independence, by allowing them to make decisions about their education for themselves. It built problem solving skills by seeing how we all confront challenges and overcome them.

These are the skills that contribute to a person being broadly educated, with or without qualifications. Qualifications are perhaps even a much smaller part than we've formerly acknowledged.

The definition of education in the dictionary is: 'showing evidence of having been taught or instructed; cultivated; cultured'. 'Displaying culture, taste and knowledge'.

It's the cultured part of education schools pay too little attention to, in the sense of seeing that other human qualities and attributes are cultured as well as knowledge.

It is something that is quite difficult to define but I know when I see it. I know that whether I consider a person to be educated or not is as much to do with *how they behave* as it is to do with what they know.

As we have been home educating, we have watched the way other children learn. We have seen these children develop skills, increase knowledge, develop their intelligence, become communicative, simply through the diverse experiences and relationships they've had.

They have become educated, most of them without schools or teachers or outcomes or agendas or formal prescriptive academics, although more formal study was applied when necessary to help move them towards the set outcomes they chose as they got older. Mostly they learnt just by living an ordinary life, in fairly ordinary ways, by being personally nurtured. And by being with caring adults.

With our own children, we have nurtured learning within them as we have nurtured care and respect and love and understanding. We have nurtured love of learning, love of one another.

We haven't pushed them systematically through any kind of agenda that was outside of their immediate need. This is not to say that we haven't made them do various tasks, practised skills, encouraged them to gain certain knowledge and seek out information, use timetables and schedules and courses as tools to help us achieve certain things at certain times. But they weren't the unquestioned norm; we discussed their purpose. We used a variety of methods over the years and discarded just as many.

For what seemed to happen when methods outside their immediate personal needs were involved was that we ended up concentrating on the *outcome* of those methods and forgetting our *original educational intention*; to raise educated, caring people rather than just people with qualifications.

Prescriptive methods resulted in us force-feeding education, instead of leading them to become educated for themselves. For, actually, children —anyone—*can* become educated for themselves.

Children enter the world wanting to become educated because they want to become part of the adult world. Most home educators I know simply educate by nurturing that desire.

And it's being educated for themselves, for their own reasons, which develops truly educated people instead of people who are educated because others are forcing them to. That approach creates resistance to true education.

To be educated you need to understand what education is for *in your own heart, for yourself.* And that comes from an open and honest and respectful education. Not one-sided, academic instruction.

I am not alone in thinking our own children have become educated people, even though I'm obviously biased; other people think it too! They are starting their working life knowing themselves, striving and achieving still, learning all the time still, and feeling fairly happy and confident.

And it was home education that got them there as I'm sure home educating will for you and yours.

Home educating is obviously not the answer for all. But it is the answer for many. It is not an easy, risk free path with guaranteed outcomes, but neither is school. However, I think it gave our children, and the others we know, a much better chance at a personal education and development which every child should really have.

Education is for the *whole person*. It should only ever be holistic and personal and enable that whole person to behave and live in a way that makes them happy, able to integrate within the world and community, gain work that they enjoy, feel their life enhanced and be successful on their own terms.

What else would it be for?

A Few Final Tips

I hope some of the stories here have given you encouragement and inspiration.

Home educating was never likely to be one simple smooth ride. Schooling isn't. Life isn't. Maybe this book will become a place to dip into when you need reassurance about your own journey.

Sometimes, when things aren't going quite as easily as you'd like, it helps to have something to turn to. But just in case you don't want a long read, below are a few quick tips, as I found that often, when I was wobbling, it could be the simplest of things that would change my outlook. Here is a reminder of some of them:

- Talk to someone, ring someone up, and share your troubles.

- Relax; it's better for you, better for the kids.

- Look after yourself as well as the children; address your needs too. Take time for you.

- You're doing this for the longer term gain, as well as the here and now. Balance the two.

- Bad days are nothing to worry about—kids have bad days in schools.

- Remember your core intentions and stick to them.

- Avoid comparing yourself to others, especially school others.

- Keep your focus on your child's needs now.

- Everything always changes. Sometimes overnight!

- Kids learn loads from playing or occupying themselves.

- Don't be afraid to give up on a day—it won't damage the kids.

- Enjoy yourselves—education is more effective as such.

- You don't always have to be in charge.

- Learn in ways that suit your child and family, not ways that prove anything to others.

- Whatever your child cannot do now is not going to be forever.

- Get out most days, for the kids and for yourself.

- Connect with others, online and physically, regularly.

- Remain flexible. Resistance is the outcome of inflexibility.

- Practise letting go of the unimportant. Only a few things really matter.

- Avoid being corrupted by mainstream thinking.

- Things constantly change; they need to, as the kids do.

- Re-examine what you're doing constantly—sometimes the kids need something different and you've missed it!

- Build your own strategies to help keep you confident. For example, look back at what you've achieved, keep photos of activities, think how your kids have grown.

- Trust that it will work out well in the end. There's proof in all those others who have gone before.

- Educate with the heart as well as the head.

- Ignore your worries for now and put the kettle on!

Lightning Source UK Ltd.
Milton Keynes UK
UKOW05f0039181116
287960UK00018B/597/P

9 780993 261428